The
West Indian Scene

by G. ETZEL PEARCY

The Geographer
U. S. Department of State

A SEARCHLIGHT ORIGINAL

D. VAN NOSTRAND COMPANY, INC.
PRINCETON, NEW JERSEY

TORONTO   LONDON

NEW YORK

D. VAN NOSTRAND COMPANY, INC.
120 Alexander St., Princeton, New Jersey
(*Principal Office*)
24 West 40 Street, New York 18, New York

D. VAN NOSTRAND COMPANY, LTD.
358, Kensington High Street, London, W.14, England

D. VAN NOSTRAND COMPANY (Canada), LTD.
25 Hollinger Road, Toronto 16, Canada

PRINTED IN THE UNITED STATES OF AMERICA

Preface

THIS book points a finger at the West Indies—our neighbors. At first from without, and then from within, the some 40,000 following words comprise that choice of facts, descriptions, evaluations, and side comments which in the author's experience best reveal a balanced picture of the West Indian scene.

How do these islands appear to Americans, each with his special set of interests? How well endowed with physical resources are the islands themselves? Can the human resources cope with the problems and crises of the region and still come up with progressive action in a tumultuous modern world? These questions and many more lie in the path the reader must tread in seeking enlightenment on the subject at hand.

By a slow spin of a globe one sees the West Indian islands making up one of three great tropical archipelagos. The other two, the East Indies and the Philippine islands, lie on the opposite side of the world. Of the three island groups only the West Indies stand as a heterogeneous collection of political entities peopled from diverse areas in five continents. In Indonesia, occupying most of the East Indies, and in the Philippines, limited entirely to a single sovereign state, a decree issued by the central government at least reverberates to the outer periphery of its archipelago. Not so in the West Indies, where nine flags flap in the Trade Winds within the relatively narrow confines of fragmented bits of land. All of the islands of the Caribbean together comprise a land area considerably less than that of the Philippines and less than one-sixth that of Indonesia. Yet politically and culturally the West Indian archipelago is highly intricate, made so largely by its position as the approach to the New World in an Age of Exploration.

For more than four centuries men of great energy streamed to

4

this focal area, creating eddies in the international train of events in their time. It is to this period of explosive action that one must turn to find many of the explanations for the situation as it exists today. Political, economic, language, religious, and cultural patterns run tangential from island to island. But despite this diversity governments and individuals on this complex of islands face many of the same problems and may take similar steps to resolve them. Indeed, the West Indian islands have been cited as a geographical laboratory in which one may study the superimposition of a range of economic, political, and social patterns upon a striking physical environment.

A number of people kindly contributed to the narrative of this book by their encouragement, suggestions, and contributions. Among them the author especially wishes to acknowledge two fellow federal geographers: Mr. David F. Naley for his assistance on the two chapters about West Indians, and Mr. Arthur P. Biggs for his compilation of area and population statistics used in the tables and text. And to Miss Clara M. Hankins, artist-cartographer, goes credit for a return to hand lettering on maps. In a more lengthy preface many others would be cited, including Florence Elizabeth Pearcy, who never once molested the 16 piles of documentation representing the 16 following chapters.

G. Etzel Pearcy

Washington, D.C.

Contents

1   *Viewpoints*

T<small>HE</small> continental vastness of the United States in the mid-latitudes makes the presence of a string of tropical isles off its shore difficult to appreciate. The West Indies possess physical and human characteristics sharply contrasting to what is normally accepted as American. Instead of broad expanses of territory the islands are limited in extent, in some cases minute in proportions. Instead of changeable weather brought by the never-ending west-to-east succession of cyclonic storms the islands lie under the monotonously steady influence of the Trade Winds and a high sun. Instead of a culture dominated by unity of purpose the islands hold a variegated array of cultures, often at cross purposes one with another.

When travelers from the United States cross the boundary into Canada, they usually fail to sense any marked contrast in either the physical environment or cultural pattern. When they cross the Rio Grande and enter Latin America to the south, the inhabitants encountered conform to a different cultural pattern, but the spacious dry Mexican landscape is strongly reminiscent of the Great Southwest left behind, stretching from western Texas to southern California. Or, when Americans cross oceans as broad as the Atlantic or Pacific, they would indeed be disappointed not to find new scenes and intriguingly different cultures. But the short hop southeastward to the West Indian islands brings them straightway into an exotic world filled with strangers.

Failure to understand the West Indies and their inhabitants is certainly no reflection against the attitudes and intentions of the American people. Rather, it is a testimony to the unusual structures of human society which have been built upon an unusual insular landscape. Just as a city motorist may drive through an unfamiliar rural setting without being aware of the life and problems of the farmers he sees, so may the average traveler superficially view the West Indies. For those who do not visit the region it becomes even more difficult to get a true perspective from the printed page or color photograph.

Following are two brief excerpts about Haiti, taken from sources with specific points of view:

> Haiti is different, exciting, scenic, memorable. It stands apart as an independent and progressive nation that blends in perfect harmony the cultures, traditions and beauties of Europe, Africa and the New World. Uncrowded, unspoiled Haiti is full of surprises and the constant contrast is a delight to the eyes and imagination: Modern and primitive intermingling . . . Cadillacs vie with burros in the bustling traffic . . . modern villas . . . gingerbread French Colonial homes . . . Kraal-like huts of native villages.

> Health conditions in Haiti are sufficiently bad so that they must be viewed as a genuine bar to development. . . . A lack of [health] facilities, and a level of accompanying illness, malnutrition, and malaise, make the people of Haiti incapable of generating development on any scale at present. Tuberculosis, malaria, and dysentery are frighteningly common. Probably only a small percentage of the population does not suffer from chronic malnutrition.

The first excerpt comes from a travel folder prepared by the *Commissariat National du Tourisme, République d'Haiti*. The second, dealing with one of the numerous problems facing the country, was written by a scholar experienced in research in this part of the world.*

It is impossible to say that one or the other of the two excerpts deliberately misrepresents what goes on in Haiti. A tourist stepping off the plane or ship at Port-au-Prince will likely be enchanted with what he sees. A scientist who probes into the plight of the less fortunate Haitians will find that ugliness is present in copious meas-

* Sidney W. Mintz, *Report on Haiti* (1959). Released in mimeographed form by the Institute of Caribbean Studies, San Juan, Puerto Rico.

Figure 1

ure. As it happens, whether fortunately or unfortunately may be a moot question, there are more tourists than scientists who visit Haiti.

The West Indian scene puts up many fronts to those who would observe it. In order to point up some contrasting impressions the next sections of this chapter will present eight distinctly different viewpoints which may be directly derived from association with the colorful tropical landscape.

Island Paradise.   Tourism runs riot in the Caribbean. Planes and cruise ships carry eager Americans by the hundreds of thousands to the islands. Some communities, such as Montego Bay, Nassau, and St. Thomas, are geared almost exclusively to tourist life. Fun in the sun has a great appeal which can be splashed in color on a million travel folders. Results of exotic tourist itineraries reflect heavily in the economic life of the islands. At the same time a certain amount of orientation is taking place. Thousands of Americans are becoming aware of the physical existence of the islands even though many see no farther than the hotel lobby or the palms that wave along the fringe of the Hilton-land promenade.

Pageant of the Past. If we believe history books, the West Indies for more than four centuries witnessed a kaleidoscopic sequence of action, intrigue-laden and endowed with many aspects of pageantry. Examined more closely and shed of romantic overtones, the adventures of high-booted conquistadores in the New World appear more starkly realistic. Subsequent times were likewise grim in most instances. Early rulers from across the sea always directed their greatest efforts toward filling their own coffers at whatever the cost to the local populace. Eras of prosperity have been numbered; troublous times plentiful. Oppression, revolution, and mass killings have taken a tragic toll among the islanders, while an underriding poverty for the common man has equated with a type of economic depression not explained away by the modern cyclical theory.

Despite the fury of the past centuries the chronicles of West Indian history leave us with many exciting notions of the development of the region. Cruelty and turmoil in retrospect tend to lose some of their savagery. We may turn back the pages of history at century intervals to catch glimpses of some of the highlights leading up to the West Indian scene of today.

Five hundred years ago the Caribbean islands were sparsely inhabited by Indians who evidently did not have much to offer to the world in which they lived. Little is written of the aborigines of that period, a primitive people who eked out an existence in the simplest way. Entirely lacking was any civilization measuring up to that which flourished in the enlightened Mayan, Aztec, or Inca eras on the neighboring mainland.

Four hundred years ago the Pinta, the Niña, and the Santa Maria had come and gone, bringing in their wake shiploads of adventure-hungry and gold-greedy Spaniards. First contacts with the Indians by Columbus and his companions had been friendly enough, but initial relations soon deteriorated into hatred and contempt as attempts were made to put the Caribs and Arawaks to work for the economic gain of the Spanish. The Arawaks, mild by nature, soon succumbed to the harsh treatment; the Caribs, being a hardier breed, savagely resisted slavery and to a degree were able to survive by taking to the hills. In the budding Age of Discovery Spain had made a clean sweep in this part of the world.

Three hundred years ago the English, French, and Dutch had become involved in Caribbean strategy. In particular they filled the vacuum in the smaller, eastern islands which the Spanish had for the most part by-passed. Most spectacular, however, was the piracy which blossomed forth in Caribbean waters. In those nostalgic days the famous sea was known as the *Spanish Main*. Actually, the term refers to the coast of South America from Panama to the mouth of the Orinoco River in Venezuela, but writers have popularized it to include any part of the Caribbean where the skull-and-crossbones flag appeared. An era of freebooting, sanctioned by the British Crown after the outbreak of war with Spain, brought "official" raids on Spanish colonial cities and shipping. Drake, Hawkins, and Cavendish were among those who excelled in sacking towns or holding them for ransom. Naturally such a lucrative occupation had an appeal to other than representatives of the British Government. The day was not long in coming when pirate ships operated by private enterprise. They might well have been scheduled, so well did they connect with the ships of the "plate fleet" making the run to Spain.

Two hundred years ago Spain had fallen upon evil days. Trouble on several scores had developed on the home front, especially with France and England. Preoccupied with trying to avoid being ground to pieces on her own continent, she relaxed her attention to the immense battery of colonies in the New World across the Atlantic. Resulting loss of control helped pave the road to independence which the colonies were to follow in a few decades.

One hundred years ago saw the big independence movement of Latin America well under way, acutely reflected in the West Indies. Revolutionists in Haiti had already eliminated French control and in 1804 established a sovereign state, setting up a precedent not only for the West Indies, but for all of Spanish and Portuguese America. Santo Domingo soon followed by shaking off the shackles of Spain, but Cuba was to wait for the best part of another half century before hoisting its own flag. Even then, because of large-scale American sugar interests, it was hair-trigger politics as to whether the Cuban national capital would be Havana or Washington. The remaining islands continued their lot as possessions of the United States and, excluding Spain, those European countries in control at the time—a role which with variations they played until the recent upsurge of independence movements gave them autonomy or sovereignty of their own.

Regardless of its implications, the effect of a history so replete with dynamic action close to the United States cannot be discounted. Even facts distorted by time provide Americans with one phase of the existing plethora of knowledge about the West Indian scene.

Source of Commodities. Rather interestingly, most of the agricultural products which leave the West Indies as exports qualify as those pleasant to the taste; they exude an aura of luxury. Sugar, cacao, coffee, bananas, pineapples, and limes tend to strike one's fancy much more than would items such as beans, rice, copra, and tubers, which normally bring forth a dull sensory reaction. Too, tobacco is associated with pleasure and leisure time, while the more potent spices, rum, arrowroot, and angostura bitters add further to the exotic list. It is quite natural that Americans associate various of these commodities with the islands of their source. Coffee from Haiti, cigars from Cuba, bitters from Trinidad, and sugar from almost any of the islands are examples of relationships which may be conjured up as applied geography of the West Indies.

Place for Investment. Wheels turn in the West Indies largely as the result of investment from the outside. American capital in particular has flowed in great quantities into Cuba, Haiti, the Dominican Republic, Puerto Rico, the Virgin Islands, and to a certain extent into the British, French, and Dutch areas—including Jamaica and Trinidad and Tobago, which were formerly British.

American financiers think of the area in terms of sugar money, banana money, shipping money, construction money, and, in fact, money for almost anything that can be linked with big business. To the uninitiated the amounts may be staggering. The American and Foreign Power Company, a U.S. concern, in the ten years prior to 1959 expended in Cuba about $190 million for improvement and expansion of its utilities installations. The dazzling string of luxury hostelries erected from Havana to Port of Spain sprang largely from American capital, with funding and accounting techniques not far different from those which erected big hotels in Miami, Cincinnati, and Phoenix. Political turmoil may intermittently slacken this type of enterprise, but nonetheless over the years a large number of Americans have learned at least a little about the West Indian scene because of its relation to their pocketbook.

Strategic Area. That the West Indies lend themselves to military strategy becomes apparent to anyone concerned with or interested in that science. Even an elementary school textbook will point out that the islands stand as natural sentinels to the Atlantic entrance of the Panama Canal. Maintenance of a two-ocean navy was long considered a necessity. One of the nightmares of both world wars was the presence, or even the fear, of German submarines in the area.

The World War II saga of exchanging outmoded warships for lend-lease bases in the British West Indies testifies to the concern with which this danger was viewed. Since the war the American Navy has been scheduling some of its most important maneuvers in the Caribbean. The great base at Guantanamo Bay stands as the focal point for these events. A recent development has been the utilization of islands in the Bahama group, along the northern fringe of the West Indies, as missile tracking stations. Americans cannot fail to be cognizant, in at least some degree, of the portentous significance which the Caribbean waters to the southeast have for national defense.

Underdeveloped Area. Despite the tourist props in the West Indies and a veneer of wealth on exhibit by a fortunate few, one cannot be blind to the fact that the area is crowded with desperately poor people. Some islands are worse off than others, but economic and social accounts become almost monotonous with discussions of population pressure, poor housing, low income figures, and distressing health conditions. Though they may seem unreal in a strange locale under the tropical sun, the tourist at least sees miserable huts crowded with ill-clad adults and children. Enroute from hotel to airport in a taxi or a rented automobile he passes picturesque though pitiful market places where venders may crouch beside nothing more than a small pile of sugar cane stalks or a heap of rice. The farmers that he sees, should he travel the countryside, bear little resemblance to those in his native land who race to town each Saturday afternoon in oversized Buicks. While Americans can look to almost any segment of the world and find poverty, they find it here so very close to home.

Political Testing Ground. Time and again political events direct attention to the West Indies. Too often the occasion bespeaks tumultuous demonstrations and attempts at sudden reform. But in recent years constructive programs aimed at political stability and betterment of the lives of the people have made impressive advances. The Cuban revolution of 1959 vigorously undermines any theory of progress in this direction, but one may view positive evidence in the improvement of the political climate in the Dominican Republic with the elimination of outright dictatorship in favor of a more representative government, and in the granting of independence to Jamaica and Trinidad and Tobago. Whatever the cause, political instability has exacted a colossal toll in privation and misery from a large percentage of the West Indian population.

The small size of the political units in the West Indies tends to magnify internal troubles, giving to routine political movement as well as revolution a sort of window-box quality. In size Haiti compares closely with Maryland, while Cuba—the giant of the Greater Antilles—is exceeded by any one of our continental states west of the Mississippi River. Among the dependencies in the region individual islands seem miniature indeed. Montserrat, a British colony, is only half again as large as Manhattan, smallest of the five boroughs making up New York City. How could even a whispering campaign go unnoticed within such restricted dimensions?

As in some other parts of the world the trend of political development in the West Indian region is toward self-rule in the dependencies and self-determinism in the republics. Desire for economic as well as political independence may be the means of stirring up unrest. The struggles in the Caribbean are watched with more than casual interest; international order finds a testing ground in these fragments of land scattered in the sea.

Cultural Museum. Into the West Indies have come people from many quarters of the world, bringing their own languages, creeds, and traditions. Only a handful of the original inhabitants survived the migratory waves that by now have just about filled the islands. Though a meeting place of far-flung cultures, the region does not necessarily function as a melting pot. No common culture of note has evolved other than that dictated by economic necessity.

Spanish, English, French, and Dutch all have official status on various of the islands, while an assortment of minority languages and dialects add to the polyglot effect. In addition to the religions associated with Spanish, English, French, and Dutch colonization one finds small segments of the Hindu and islamic worlds in Trinidad as well as expressions of strange cults among the Negroes. The practice of Voodooism, originating in West Africa, is associated with Haiti. This type of exotic culture appeals to most Americans as a highly colorful type of festive entertainment along with the Limbo and Calypso.

The color question also uniquely asserts itself in the West Indies. Through the centuries a large and continuous intermingling among Europeans, Negroes, and, to a much lesser extent, Indians, has ultimately produced a gradation of color rather than sharply defined categories. A small percentage of the population is pure white, a somewhat greater percentage pure black, but the majority have mixed blood, expressed ethnically as Mestizo. Color gradation is found not only from island to island, but usually within the confines of any single island. It is commonly accepted that in most of the West Indies anyone is "white" unless he is literally black—just the reverse of the prevailing attitude in the United States.

PROBLEMS TO IDENTIFY AND RESOLVE

Each of the viewpoints presented above gives some notion—admittedly superficial—of isolated characteristics typical of the West Indies and West Indian life. The task at hand is to merge the individual facets of the West Indian scene and thereby gain a broad overview. No one issue can be allowed to predominate at the expense of obscuring others; rather a balance must be struck to bring each issue into proper focus. For example, realistic questions may be posed which draw upon facts from a range of viewpoints. How may a traveler in the West Indies see beneath the veneer of tourism? How may the scholar see the past in proper perspective? What constitutes a sound investment in the West Indies? How can West Indian islands best be encompassed into the U.S. defense area without infringement of their sovereign rights? How can such small political units be encouraged to maintain and develop their autonomy with dignity?

Essentially, most of the evils now plaguing the various West Indian islands could be assaulted, with chances of success, by resolving the following four problems:

(1) Overcrowding, or *population pressure;*

(2) Bad or ineffective government, or *political pressure;*

(3) Inequality in land tenure and opportunity, or *social pressure;* and

(4) Lack of full scale development, or *economic pressure.*

Raising the standard of living and bringing about stability hinge on success or failure in attacking such problems and remedying deep-seated maladjustments. One may safely predict that the most successful assaults upon these fearsome problems will come from within the region.

2

Between Two Continents

Some Australians refer to the East Indies area as the *Near North*. In the same vein Americans might look upon the West Indian region as the *Near South*. The short distance across the Straits of Florida from United States territory to West Indian islands admits of such a term. A scant 100 miles separates Key West from Havana, while the luxurious Bahamian resorts of the Biminis lie less than 50 miles to the east of Miami Beach. Also significant, the expression "overseas" seldom applies to tourist travel to even those parts of the West Indies most remote from continental United States.

Washing the shores of most West Indian islands, the Caribbean Sea, along with the Gulf of Mexico, not infrequently gives the impression of being an American Mediterranean, a name pointing up its mid-position between two continental land masses (see Figure 1). A straight line drawn from the center of the North American continent to the center of the South American continent squarely bisects the Caribbean Sea.

Regional Names and Identification. Terminology by which to identify and discuss the West Indian islands, though relatively simple along broad lines, does have a number of complexities when viewed analytically. The most appropriate overall name for the region, *The West Indies,* was also adopted in 1957 as the official title for a federation of 10 British colonies in the Caribbean, even to the extent of turning the initial "The" into a proper noun (like the "El" of El Salvador). Although the federation fell apart in 1962 the association of its name with the area remains, creating a certain amount of confusion. Thus, reference to the West Indian *islands, region,* or *realm* avoids the difficulty of distinguishing the more limited political from the broad geographic connotation, though in some instances the context makes the meaning clear.

The Caribbean islands serves as a synonym to and for the West Indian islands, although the archipelago forms only the northern and eastern limits of the sea. In contrast, a similar term, *Caribbean America,* includes not only the West Indian islands, but also Central America and Mexico to the west and sometimes all or a part of Colombia and Venezuela on the South American mainland. *Middle America* has roughly the same meaning as Caribbean America, but no such term as "Middle American islands" exists.

Still another key word is *Antilles,* which appeared on maps from as early as the 14th century to identify certain imaginary islands thought to lie in the Atlantic Ocean between Portugal and Cipango, the latter term equating with Japan. After the actual discovery of the West Indian islands by European explorers, the term lingered. Today, however, Antilles as an overall term for the archipelago finds little usage. Rather, the large islands of Cuba, Hispaniola, Jamaica, and Puerto Rico are called the *Greater Antilles* (see Figure 2); the remaining smaller islands to the south and east, from the Virgin Islands to Trinidad, are called the *Lesser Antilles* (see Figure 3). The Dutch use the term as part of the official name for their West Indian islands: Netherlands Antilles.

The major chain of the Lesser Antilles is further subdivided into the *Windward* and *Leeward islands.* The Leeward group comprises Guadeloupe and islands to the north. Southward, the Windwards extend from Dominica to Grenada, excluding Barbados, Trinidad, and Tobago which lie askew to the alignment of the main chain. Until 1958 these climatic terms were utilized by the British to define political areas: Leeward Islands Colony and Windward Islands Colony. Logic fails in this nomenclature, for both groups lie in the very teeth of the Northeast Trades.

It proves virtually impossible to determine by geographical definition any precise delineation of the West Indian islands. In the southern Caribbean a number of islands closely parallel the coast of South America. Among them the three principal islands of the

Netherlands Antilles along with Trinidad and Tobago definitely belong to the West Indian group. But squarely between Bonaire and Trinidad lie others, including the sizable Isla de Margarita (over which Venezuela has sovereign control), which are seldom if ever considered as West Indian units. Near the western limit of the Caribbean a few scattered islands belong to Colombia, Honduras, Nicaragua, and the United States, some of which are subject to dispute. In a narrow sense they are not West Indian, though often they are spoken of as such in a broad sense or blanketed by the term Caribbean islands.

To the north of the main axis of the West Indian archipelago the Bahama Islands lie entirely in Atlantic waters. Nevertheless, the Bahamas are accepted by some as West Indian, or Caribbean, islands. They bring land areas of the archipelago 275 miles farther north than would otherwise be the case and account for the only part of the West Indian region lying north of the Tropic of Cancer. Far to the north, some 700 miles off the Carolina coast, the Bermuda Islands cannot possibly be construed as West Indian. Yet they may be found associated with the Bahamas and other British West Indian areas for the sake of convenience, as in statistical lists, yearbooks, or, for that matter, anywhere to avoid a more detailed breakdown.

Thus delineated, with a fuzzy perimeter in places, the main chain of West Indian islands forms an arc through approximately 25 degrees of longitude (1,675 miles) and 13 degrees of latitude (900 miles). If the western tip of Cuba were placed on the map of the United States at San Francisco, the archipelago would swing east and south with Trinidad superimposed upon the Texas port of Galveston.

Early Regional Role. By its location the West Indian region offered the first approach to a restless Europe in search of new worlds. The ships of Columbus, powered by the Trade Winds west and south across the Atlantic, were only the beginning of a stream which for more than three centuries reached Western Hemisphere lands. The Spanish Main earned its fabled reputation as the grooved path through Caribbean waters at the western end of this transoceanic route. Only later did the now important routes from Europe's western ports to the east coasts of North America and South America develop. Although ships and planes still make their way across the Atlantic directly to West Indian ports and airfields, the modern version of this middle route cannot offer much competition with those to the north and south.

The Isthmus of Panama initially endowed the West Indian islands with their role as a crossroads. Long before the opening of the Panama Canal the narrow strip of land connecting North and South America became a natural point of portage between the oceans. Since the Caribbean Sea with its islands lay directly between Europe and the Isthmus, the route to the Pacific could hardly by-pass the archipelago. During a period of nearly two centuries, from 1561 to 1740, Spain required that traffic from Europe bound for Spanish South America enter the continent at specific points, such as Callao, the port for Lima. This itinerary, though geographically impractical, required transit across the narrow neck of Panama to avoid the dangerous passage around Cape Horn. This situation obviously stimulated the importance of the West Indies. The accident of location had somewhat the same effect here as in the Middle East, which long benefited from its position as a transit zone between Europe and the Orient. Commerce flowing north and south intersected that moving east and west through the Caribbean, en route from one American continent to the other. The rugged terrain of the Caribbean's mainland shores prevented travel by land except as a supplement to that by water, accounting still further for the early development of the West Indies as a kind of primitive entrepôt.

Its roles as a transit area and as a crossroads by no means detracted from the traffic destined to and stemming from the West Indian area itself. In fact, the exchange of goods between the old world and the new and from one American continent to the other stimulated regional trade. Islands strung for hundreds of miles through the sea could only be logical stops along shipping lanes. Provisioning for sailing ships and coaling stations for steamships, as well as regional and local commerce, contributed to the building up of dozens of busy ports. No other means of communication existed for the individual islands, either with the outside world or with each other. After the Canal was cut across the Isthmus of Panama, traffic between the Atlantic and Pacific sharply increased, continuing to assure the crossroads role of the West Indian area. Shipping from the east coast of North America to the west coasts of both Americas figured prominently in establishing well traveled sea lanes.

Re-orientation. Air transportation brought yet a new dimension into the ever-changing route pattern to and through the West Indian region. Aircraft in the 1930's were incapable of long flights without refueling stops. Thus, islands became stepping stones on commercial air routes penetrating or traversing the area. In 1930 Pan American Airways developed a trunk route from Miami to San Juan with stops in Santiago de Cuba, Port-au-Prince, and Santo Domingo City. Previous to that time the most satisfactory passenger service between the two latter cities was by boat via New York City! And so new lines of communication were laid down over an area easy of access but badly handicapped by lack of interregional transport. The same stepping-stones type of air service exists today, but as local schedules by relatively small planes. With long distance nonstop flights now possible, trunk routes to the West Indian islands bring planes directly from the outside, as from New York to Montego Bay or Miami to San Juan. Or, the big planes may make a single stop or overfly the area entirely in linking the United States with continental South America.

Distance of the West Indian islands one from another has played a prime part in their development. The large number of islands, separated by intervening water passages of 20, 30, and 40 or more miles in width, resulted to a great extent in the growth of individual communities. Each island, along with any nearby satellites, formed the basis for a colony. Ferry service so typical of other insular areas in the world never became established here. Perhaps a more sedentary type of colonization void of hostile international competition might have provided closer interisland ties. Moreover, multiple water passages allowed free entry to and through the West Indian islands without navigational limitation. Windward Passage between

Cuba and Hispaniola and Mona Passage between Puerto Rico and Hispaniola are the best known of the entrances to Caribbean waters. Along with numerous others they have greatly handicapped any effective "bottling-up" or blockading of shipping.

Within the last few years the spacing of the West Indian islands, especially those of the Lesser Antilles, has taken on new significance. International concern over the law of the sea indicates the advantage of standardizing the breadth of a territorial sea along all coasts, including those of islands. To date the states of the world disagree on the breadth. Maritime states, believing in freedom of the seas, claim a three-(nautical)-mile territorial sea. At the other extreme many states claim 12 miles, thereby extending sovereign control of offshore water areas at the expense of the high seas. For example, no high-seas passage would exist along the 300-mile stretch between Guadeloupe and Grenada should a 12-mile territorial sea be universally adopted. As should be readily apparent, any curtailment of high seas, particularly in critical ocean lanes, impedes U.S. national defense by restricting maneuverability of naval ships and flexibility of the merchant marine. This key issue is discussed later in the chapter in relation to American defense in the Caribbean.

MILITARY IMPLICATIONS OF LOCATION

The position of the West Indian islands automatically encompasses them within any defense plans or patterns which the United States can possibly devise. No region in the Western Hemisphere other than on American soil itself offers comparable strategic implications to the nation's military security. The Monroe Doctrine, dating back to 1823, was the first significant expression of international complications involving trans-Atlantic powers. It was formulated primarily to stay disruptive European influence in the Caribbean area. At that time the dangers of overseas incursions were perhaps as imminent, but certainly no more perilous than they appear to be now. The strategic implications of the nearby West Indian region conceivably were clear to American diplomats of nearly a century and a half ago. Nevertheless, it must be remembered that the Monroe Doctrine side-steps European influence in the Western Hemisphere to the extent that both insular and mainland colonies of the British, French, Dutch, Spanish, and Danish remained unaffected. In fact, it was British naval power that supported the policy and vouchsafed its success. Opening of the Panama Canal to traffic in August 1914 was the next major testimony to our awareness of the paramount importance of southern waters to any defense system. Again the Caribbean was a prime factor in this development, the West Indian islands unquestionably assuming the role of sentinels guarding the eastern approaches to the Canal.

New Menaces—New Defenses. Not until World War I did the American nation experience serious military hazards of an enemy operation in nearby waters. German submarines, as they menaced shipping off the immediate Atlantic and Gulf coasts of the United States, were with only minor exceptions the only instance since early colonial struggles which brought actual warfare from across the sea to the country's very doorstep. The same evil again presented itself during World War II, prompting the American acquisition of five bases in the West Indies on British territory. Fifty destroyers were exchanged for 99-year leases to these bases. The transaction seemed to catch the public eye, receiving a tremendous amount of publicity.

The bases fitted into a double defense zone set up through the West Indies to guard the Panama Canal and thereby maintain an effective two-ocean navy, and also to thwart submarine attacks on shipping (see Figure 4). The main, or inner, zone pivoted on Guantanamo Bay, San Juan, and the newly acquired base on Trinidad. Subsidiary to these bases was the new one established at Kingston. The four Greater Antillean islands plus Trinidad made up the principal line of defense. A secondary, or outer, zone supported the first as an auxiliary, stretching from the coast of Florida to that of Venezuela through the Bahamas, the Virgin Islands, and continuing through the Lesser Antilles. Three of the new bases in this chain—Exuma, Antigua, and St. Lucia—were the mainstays of the outer defense. Because of their location the islands could block off the Caribbean against enemy undersea craft and maintain watch over the passages between islands.

Peacetime Alert. In 1960 four of the lend-lease bases again came into the limelight. After only 17 years of the 99 had passed, the United States agreed to relinquish about four-fifths of the total area encompassed by the bases, amounting to 77 out of 96 square miles. Only specific functions of a military nature were to remain. The agreement reached with the United Kingdom and with local governmental representatives provided, in brief, for the retention of:

1. A naval station at Chaguaramas on Trinidad to carry on defense and electronic research missions;

2. Limited installations at St. Lucia, including use of an airfield;

3. Use of an airfield and two radar sites on Antigua and facilities for space exploration; and

4. A small area near Kingston for defense use, later relinquished.

These arrangements were to remain in force until 1977, continuing after that only by mutual agreement. However, in 1962 the installations on Trinidad and Jamaica were accepted by the governments of these two new sovereign states. In addition other defense installations, under various agreements, have more recently sprung up in the Caribbean area—for example, weather stations and oceanographic research stations.

In peacetime the Caribbean serves as one of the principal Atlantic Fleet Training Areas. In wartime it is converted into a series of routes over which a major quantity of petroleum and other products reach the United States. Lack of protection thus means the danger of ships being sunk. Naval operations in the area, in order to provide the necessary protection, have a defense system consisting of several key and auxiliary installations. The base at Chaguaramas, already mentioned, is for the support of surface and air operations. The principal naval station is situated in southern Cuba at Guantanamo Bay, ranking along with the station at Newport News, Virginia, for training purposes. More recently, Roosevelt Road in Puerto Rico has been developed into a major fleet training facility. A smaller naval station at San Juan is the headquarters of the Naval District Commandant and Commander of the Caribbean Sea Frontier. Finally, the eastern half of the small island of Vieques, 10 miles east of Puerto Rico, was selected as an amphibious training area. Somewhat incongruous to the utilization of the island for this grim practice was the construction there of an elaborate luxury hotel.

A further link in the West Indian defense system is Ramey Air Force Base, on the extreme northwest corner of Puerto Rico. As a part of the Strategic Air Command its objectives encompass an area far wider than the Caribbean. The base likewise guards the Panama Canal, though this function is less important than it would have been even a decade ago.

Reflecting the space age, U.S. military installations in the West Indian region also include a chain of stations for tracking and monitoring missiles launched from Patrick Air Force Base at Cape Kennedy. Grand Bahama, Eleuthera, San Salvador (Watling Island), Grand Turk, Antigua, Trinidad, and other islands are all equipped with radar for this purpose. The most remote station in the chain, at Ascension Island, lies isolated in the southern Atlantic far beyond the Caribbean area.

The entire concept of defense in the Caribbean has changed since the United States acquired the bases from Britain in 1941. The Panama Canal has lost some of its military significance with the coming of missiles and rocketry. In addition, the larger naval vessels can no longer pass through the Canal. A two-ocean navy engages less concern from the Department of Defense than in the days of World War II. Nevertheless, the Canal and its Caribbean sentinels are far from being written off; their location continues to be of great significance. Because vital supplies from Latin America normally pass through West Indian waters, the routes must be kept free. In the same vein, naval ships may be needed in the area for patrol or to quell "brush-fire" disorders among Latin American states. Within the last few years Panama, Guatemala, and Honduras have all asked for assistance against revolution exported from Cuba.

Since 1958 more and more countries have been making claims for a 12-mile territorial sea. Traditionally the United States has recognized one three miles in breadth. Should offshore sovereignty be extended to 12 miles, the navy would be less effective in protecting Caribbean sea lanes in the event of hostilities. At present any water channel between islands greater than six miles (twice the breadth of the territorial sea) includes a transit area of high seas. But if a 12-mile territorial sea were recognized internationally, any channel would have to be more than 24 miles wide to allow passage through high seas. While the "rights of innocent passage" apply in territorial waters, they may easily be retracted by any sovereign power in times of international tension and trouble. Thus, submarines could use such channels unobserved, while surface craft would be obliged to avoid passing through them unless sovereignty rights were ignored.

It is unlikely that the West Indian region will lose its strategic value to the United States even though the dangers of atomic warfare lessen that value.

3

Physical Lines of an Archipelago

IT IS almost a geographic cliché to say that the West Indian islands comprise a partially submerged mountain range. Yet this concise truism affords a basic explanation of the physical environment enveloping the archipelago. Land surface and climate alike reflect an insular character. Soil, natural vegetation, and animal life likewise express the tight relationship of land to water. In fact, no point on any island is more than 55 miles from the sea. Water washing the shorelines of the islands and islets molds the coastal configuration, and air moving in from the surrounding bodies of water patterns day-to-day weather.

Land-sea relationships in the Caribbean extend far beyond physical geography. If, in relation to the bulk of land forming the West Indian islands, mean sea level had been 25 feet higher or 25 feet lower, the whole history of the region would doubtlessly have fallen into other chapters. Human occupance on all the islands has been closely associated with the harbors, narrow coastal strips, valley accesses to interior regions—in fact, to every physical feature which facilitated settlement and development. For example, the presence of rich land close to protected harbors accounted for early successes of plantation crops. It cannot be doubted that to a substantial degree the shoreline perimeter of each island influences the human environment more markedly than the towering mountains which in many instances may loom in close view.

LAND AND SEA

It is not difficult to imagine that the great arc of West Indian islands makes up a half-drowned chain of mountains which ties in with the great Western Cordillera on the North American and South American mainlands. In fact, geologists declare that at one time there may have been continuous land which stretched along the axes of the archipelago all the way from the Yucatan and Central America to the Guiana Mountains of Venezuela. Submarine contours as well as those above sea level go far to bear out this hypothesis.

Not far to the north of Puerto Rico the depth of the Atlantic reaches 30,180 feet, exceeding in vertical measurement the height of Mt. Everest. Within 60 miles of this spot, known as Milwaukee Depth, the island of Hispaniola reaches elevations of over 10,000 feet—the equivalent of a cordillera of more than 40,000 feet in height. In other West Indian areas, too, the bottom of the Atlantic Ocean and Caribbean Sea may be measured in miles. South of Cuba, for example, a long narrow undersea gorge extends for hundreds of miles and has a maximum depth of 23,760 feet—more than four miles.

In flying over the West Indian region one is conscious of undersea topography as well as the contours of the land itself. Especially in bright sunlight the depth of the water may be seen in technicolor fashion, changes in the color of the surface forming stark, unsymmetrical patterns. Around many of the islands shallow patches show up as expanses of greenish white. In turn, deeper and deeper water shows a progression of color through light green, green, to dark blue. The degree of change depends, of course, upon how rapidly the seabed falls off. An island may have water which is deep blue right off its shore. Elsewhere near the same island, however, the floor of the sea may slope gently away from the land with the complete color range that goes with it. The clarity of the water also allows underwater coral deposits, or "heads," to be seen as dark splotches which mar the consistency of an otherwise light-colored surface.

This submarine world has a romantic as well as scientific side. Hardly 40 miles north of the Dominican Republic an area of shallow water known as Silver Bank and Navidad Bank is sur-

Europe, strove to continue the... gentlemen who would not deign t... succeeded generation, intermarriage ... has robbed the region of a clear-cut ... laboring class and a white managerial c... manual labor is beneath the dignity of the ... and continues to be in evidence. Those wh... from using their brawn, irrespective of the pre... scale.

Nevertheless, there is a gradual breaking down o... old concept. American workmen within the last deca... to Puerto Rico on construction jobs and seemed not ... their task of building modern structures. In fact, Puer... witnessing more and more "Continentals" who choose to m... way in the regular routine of the island's economy. While ... newcomers seldom work at menial jobs, they display all of ... energy needed to make a livelihood.

Even the tourist is being helped over any prejudices which he ... may hold about climate in the West Indies. Sports requiring vigor... ...us action find many challengers irrespective of the thermometer ...ading. Malarial mosquitoes, associated with the tropics at their ...orst, have been for the most part eliminated as a health hazard. ...mmer in the Caribbean Sea formerly had little appeal to the ...cationist, but air conditioning has lengthened the "season" to one ...ting throughout the year. If winter retains its greater popularity ...s largely because of the contrast between the January tempera-...e in choice spots such as Grenada or Pétionville and the chill of ... York, Chicago, and other American cities.

...imatic statistics for the West Indian region take on additional ...ning when compared to areas of higher latitude in North ...rica and Europe. Within continental United States the south-...Florida city of Key West has the only weather station never ...ding freezing temperatures or below. Conversely, no weather ...in the West Indian islands ever registers freezing.

...ile the January temperature in New York City averages an ...2° F., thermometers in Havana, San Juan, and Port of Spain

rounded by deep water, including some of the deepest in the Atlantic. Its distinctive light color causes it to stand out prominently. Here on the shallow bottom lie the remains of a great Spanish Plate Fleet, sunk in 1643 with treasure valued at some $15-20 million in gold. As one of the most famous treasure lures in the world much excitement revolved around this "golden graveyard," though most of the valuable cargo has long since been recovered.

The air traveler likewise may be impressed by the precipitous topography he sees above sea level. In places the vista appears to be nothing other than great banks of mountain walls. East of Hispaniola the West Indian archipelago is confined to a single chain of mountains, curving southward through Puerto Rico and the Lesser Antilles. But to the west three chains are distinguishable, fingering out through Cuba, Jamaica, and the small Cayman island group to reach the great Cordillera making up the backbone of Central America. Hispaniola itself presents the appearance of a complex mountain knot, actually the junction of the entire system of individual chains.

All of the Greater Antilles and five of the Lesser Antilles have mountains rising to elevations greater than 4,000 feet. In contrast, much of Cuba and eight of the more important Lesser Antilles lack characteristics of a mountainous terrain. Rather, these areas largely comprise monotonously level to rolling limestone platforms never more than a few hundred feet above the sea. In places mangrove swamps may fringe the coast, as in Trinidad. The low-lying areas somewhat detract from, but do not destroy, the mountains-in-the-sea hypothesis. Some islands may have extensive areas suitable for crop production while on other islands cultivable land may be at a premium, found only in mountain valleys or along the coastal margin. Variety of land forms from island to island, or even within the bounds of the same island, gives the region some of its more intriguing scenic aspects.

The highest and most rugged relief is to be found in Haiti and the Dominican Republic on the island of Hispaniola. Pico Duarte in the Cordillera Central of the latter country, towering to 10,300 feet, exceeds all other elevations in the West Indian region. The highest peak of Cuba, near the south coast in the Sierra Maestra, measures 8,397 feet, a thousand feet higher than Jamaica's maximum elevation in the Blue Mountains on the eastern end of the island near the city of Kingston. Because of their restricted size some of the Lesser Antilles give a striking impression of mountain mass to the voyager who approaches them by sea. For example, on the relatively tiny islands of Dominica and Martinique are mountains reaching heights of nearly 5,000 feet. On the even more diminutive Montserrat, with only 32 square miles of territory, stands a mountain of 3,000 feet. These islands are literally the tops of a great mountain chain standing on the bottom of the sea.

Geologically speaking, the West Indian islands are currently undergoing dynamic changes. In addition to the usual processes of erosion, crustal movements of the earth are forcing some of the islands up and others down in relation to sea level. Further, the tepid water of the Caribbean fosters the building of coral reefs over submerged areas around the margins of the islands. In the Lesser Antilles volcanic action is not unknown. On two consecutive days in 1902 tops blew off of Mt. Soufrière on Guadeloupe and Mt. Pelée on Martinique, the latter killing upwards of 40,000 people. Five years later, in another violent manifestation of instability, an earthquake destroyed the city of Kingston on Jamaica.

The small size of the islands precludes the presence of any rivers of consequence, as for example, permitting navigation or forming the basis for a canalized waterway net. On the other hand the mountainous terrain of the larger islands serves as a catchment basin, giving rise to streams suitable for the generation of hydroelectric energy.

The combination of sharp relief and submerged land has provided the islands with a wealth of excellent harbors. Some are formed by the fragmented slopes of volcanic craters. Even the smaller islands have the advantage of coastal indentations capable of port development. Cuba especially is favored in this respect with its succession of pouch-shaped harbors rimming the island and providing easy means of exporting sugar even in the earliest days.

CLIMATE AND ITS EFFECTS

Within the tropics. From one end of the West Indian ... the climate conforms in certain measure to a ... regional ... High, but not excessively high, temperatures, ... short-lived showers, sunny skies most of the time, and ... cooling breezes rather well describe normal sea-level con... ... Isle of Pines, the south coast of Hispaniola, Antigua, ... or that matter, any of the islands. Probably the abun... ... e and the effect of a copious rainfall on the vegetation ... area its reputation as a tropical paradise. Climatic varia... ... place to place and season to season exist, but mostly ... ...logical detail. At higher altitudes cooler temperatures p... ...and more rain falls on the windward than on the leew... ...side of mountainous islands. Snow falls but rarely on even ... highest range, nor does one need a topcoat in mid-January o... most northerly bit of land in the island group.

A tropical climate seemingly endowed with all of the prereq... for a relaxing vacation is not necessarily one to stimulate ... At least the hot humid tropics have generally been avoided ... white man who must engage in manual labor to make ... Since the West Indies lie in the tropics, they are popularly ... at least by the uninitiated, to fall into this category. How ... a concept must by no means be accepted without wei... evidence.

When the Europeans first came to the West Indies, st... the turn of the 16th century, they overlooked no op... capitalize on their newly found world. But they were ... severe shortage of labor to work the mines and man th... A slave trade bringing Negroes from the coast of ... remedied the situation. These inhabitants from ... Coast, and other sections of Africa's western coast ... Angola were well adapted to the West Indian cli... cidentally, was considerably more salubrious tha... tinental type from which they had come. In ... whites from Spain, and later from other cou...

the modern part could be wiped out. One city, Pointe-à-Pitre on the windward side of Guadeloupe, proves so inviting to hurricanes that it is being abandoned—an action strangely uncommon in most disaster areas. Unfortunately, planted crops are subject to the fury of the winds, with insurance virtually the only possible precaution to offset the financial hazard of hurricane damage.

After leaving the West Indian region hurricanes, before spending their energy, have in memorable instances wrought havoc along the Gulf Coast and in peninsular Florida. In recent years, probably in response to the retracking of upper-air jet streams, these storms more commonly swing north along the eastern seaboard of the United States. Even New England and Maritime Canada have suffered from hurricanes before they were finally dissipated at the end of their long treks. Names like Alice, Betsy, Clara, and Dolores are becoming more familiar in American news as meteorologists each season tag the onrushing storms in sequence with girl's names, arranged in alphabetical order. Meanwhile the West Indies have had no respite from the occurrence of hurricanes; they just share them more generously with their neighbors to the north and west.

THE RESOURCE BASE

When the first Spaniards came to the New World four and one-half centuries ago their appetites were whetted by the gold found first on the islands in the Caribbean and then on the mainland. They fervently sought the glittering metal on a grand scale in the Greater Antilles, but to no avail, so limited was the supply. In some instances, as on Hispaniola, a few deposits were discovered and worked. Soon the West Indies became a gateway to mineral riches on the mainland rather than a source of them.

The conquistadores, shrewd as they were and ever on the lookout to make their adventures profitable, introduced sugar in the West Indies. However, greatest interest in the establishment and operation of sugar plantations was left to the British, French, and Dutch who later capitalized on the fertile soil of the Antillean islands, especially the smaller ones. Here was started production of a commodity demanded in the advancing culture of Europe and which proved to be fully as remunerative as gold. Thus, soil and climate were the first significant expressions of resources in the archipelago. Since that time millions upon millions of tons of tropical products have been harvested and exported, exotic to peoples of a more severe environment.

Any modern inventory of natural resources in the West Indies will be impressive only if the more intangible types are included along with those that may be measured or weighed and tagged with an approximate value per unit in dollars, pounds, or pesos. For example, warm sunshine and waving palms are of the natural environment and have been skillfully exploited to bring in great tourist revenue all the way from Nassau to Port of Spain.

Only on three islands are there mineral resources of sufficient quality and quantity to merit attention from the standpoint of international significance; elsewhere mineral deposits are of local or, at best, of regional importance. First, bauxite deposits in Jamaica are credited as comprising one-fifth or more of the world total with some 300 million tons. Its discovery only dates back to World War II. Continued investigations may cause upward revision of the potential supply.

Second, on the island of Trinidad a natural deposit of asphalt, known as Pitch Lake, has no equal. Continued removal of the asphalt for the best part of a century has scarcely reduced the level thanks to replacement by seepage from underground sources of oil nearby. In addition to the viscous pitch Trinidad also possesses regular petroleum deposits, now estimated at 500 million barrels including relatively recent offshore findings. They are dwarfed by those of Venezuela, but still constitute a major field roughly comparable in production to those in nearby Colombia.

Third, the eastern end of Cuba has an assortment of minerals worthy of note. Deposits of iron ore, manganese, chrome, nickel, and copper add up to a resource potential which to date has been utilized largely as items for export. Elsewhere in Cuba are scattered minor deposits, including petroleum in a field on the north coast near Matanzas.

Heavy rainfall on mountainous terrain provides the Greater Antilles with a substantial potential for development of hydroelectric energy. However, the relatively small amount of industrialization restrict effective use of this unexpendable resource other than on Puerto Rico. For power requirements it has in the past generally been easier to import fuel with which to generate electricity, but increasing attention is being given this source of power.

Much more noteworthy than minerals beneath the surface or water tumbling down the mountainside are a series of resources which support widespread agricultural activities. Soils, a twelve-month growing season, and sufficient moisture are basic to the very existence of the region's population. These resources may be utilized for plantation culture bringing wealth to absentee owners and large corporations, or for sustaining the life of the humble peasant-type farmers on small plots of land. In Cuba especially are conditions favorable for agriculture. Only about one-fourth of the island is too mountainous or otherwise unsuited for cultivation. The remaining area of nearly level or gentle rolling relief, a little larger in size than the state of South Carolina, is overlain with fertile limestone soil particularly favorable to the growth of sugar cane or, for that matter, an almost endless array of crops. The climate matches the surface for excellence of growing conditions.

Other islands in the Caribbean have an environment no less favorable to agriculture than Cuba except in areal dimensions and, in some places, a lack of adequate rainfall. In Puerto Rico the sugar cane fields rim the island along the coastal plain. In Haiti and the Dominican Republic farmlands are more likely to penetrate the deep-cut valleys of mountainous areas.

Natural vegetation, relatively luxurious throughout the West Indies except on leeward slopes and coasts, provides only a limited resource base. Grasses support some pastoral activities, but only where they have not been squeezed out by crops. Likewise, forests have never sponsored more than a desultory secondary lumbering industry despite the rampant tree growth on wet windward slopes. The more accessible forested lands were cleared for crop production, leaving only remote areas clothed with trees. Stands of coniferous trees in the Bahama Islands are in a small way an exception to the general situation.

Tourism, certainly a leading economic activity in many parts of the West Indian region, depends as does agriculture upon a specific complement of environmental factors, each of which rightly qualifies as a natural resource. Scenery, based upon relief, distribution of land and water, and natural vegetation, makes up one important part of tourist appeal; climate, mainly warm but not excessively hot temperatures and abundant sunshine, makes up another. From this fortunate combination the hand of man seems to have an unlimited potential in building up a tourist industry. However, the economic stability of a region dependent upon relief and climate as resources in this broad sense may be subject to question. A hundred million tons of high-quality iron ore under the surface, though not so glamorous, is far less subject to the frailties of our society, economic or otherwise, for sustaining its value in the long pull.

An inventory of any region's resources is necessarily only an indication of economics in the abstract. This maxim is particularly true in the West Indies, where multifarious factors from both within and without the region intertwine to determine the use or misuse to which the resources will be put. The richest and most abundant resources may be of naught to the local populace, or the most meager of resources may be developed to improve the well-being of many. In later chapters the disposition of the resource base in the West Indian region appears in a more analytical light.

4   *The Early West Indians*

Wᴇ sᴏᴍᴇᴛɪᴍᴇs tend to believe that if Columbus, or some other European, had not discovered the "New World," it would never have existed. This strange but common egocentric view has been nurtured by the practice of beginning the study of "American History" with the arrival of the European upon the "virgin" land of the two American continents. With but a token glance at the aborigines—Araucanians, Aztecs, Iroquois, Seminoles—the student plods off across the plains with Ponce de Leon or penetrates the rugged Appalachian country with Daniel Boone.

Actually, of course, the native peoples of the Americas numbered in the millions long before the first European sailors were blown westward across the Atlantic. These millions were irregularly scattered over a vast land area, and the societies or civilizations they established were as varied as were those of their contemporaries in Europe and the Near East. On the one extreme was the highly organized Inca Empire of the Andes, with a thoroughly regimented citizenry estimated at anywhere from 3.5 to 32 million. This nation was sufficiently wealthy in both material and knowledge to develop complex agricultural practices; to build roads, bridges, temples; and to become skilled in metallurgy and weaving. At the other end of the late pre-Columbian spectrum were the small bands of nomadic hunters and gatherers dispersed from one end of the Western Hemisphere realm to the other. These Indians, or Amerindians, engaged in agriculture little more complex than picking berries and knew nothing of the arts and skills developed by the more advanced societies of the time.

Operations Aboriginal. The people of what came to be known as the West Indies fell somewhere between the two cultural extremes, although they were probably more closely akin to the simpler groups than to the monolithic empires. By the time Columbus appeared on the Caribbean scene in the latter part of the 15th century, the area was already, by pre-Columbian standards, densely populated. Estimates have placed this early population at as many as a million.

Archaeological evidence indicates that the Ciboney, or Guanahatabey, were probably the earliest, or one of the earliest, groups of people to inhabit the Antilles. The Spaniards encountered the Ciboney only in the western parts of Haiti and Cuba, but they apparently had at one time been more widely dispersed. Some scholars contend that they migrated to the islands from Florida. The Ciboney depended on hunting and fishing for a livelihood, and in many of their cultural traits probably were not unlike present-day Indian groups living in remote areas of the Amazon equatorial forests.

The Ciboney, except for a few scattered groups, were displaced by the Arawak, who probably reached the Caribbean islands from South America. It was the Arawak who first greeted—and later were eliminated by—the Spanish conquistadores throughout the Greater Antilles. Arawak groups occupied all of the major islands from the Bahamas to the Virgin Islands, including Cuba, Jamaica, Hispaniola, and Puerto Rico. Many of the Arawak lived in well-established villages, some having as many as 1,000 houses, and had developed a fairly complicated political system. The Arawak also were more advanced agriculturists than their predecessors. They were able to grow, sometimes with the aid of fertilizers and irrigation, a great variety of plants, including manioc, maize, sweet potatoes, arrowroot, beans, peppers, avocados, papayas, peanuts, pineapples, and other fruits and vegetables. Fishing apparently was not a major source of food, and hunting was even less important.

Surplus goods were traded rather widely throughout the islands and even with the mainland. Items of commerce included agricultural products, pottery, wooden bowls, and various minerals, among which were silver and gold. Specializations also developed, such as woodworking on Gonave Island off the western coast of Haiti.

The Arawak had trained warriors and a variety of weapons, including bows and poisoned arrows, in their arsenal. Nevertheless, they were no match for the warlike group known as the Carib who swept northward from the South American mainland. Carib amphibious assault teams raided the Arawak villages in the Lesser Antilles and killed the men or took them captive for later use in cannibalistic rites, while Arawak women were prized as additional wives. By 1492 the Caribs had conquered and occupied the Lesser Antilles, were raiding as far west as Jamaica, and were generally in a period of expansion.

The Carib were skilled sailors, navigators, and boatwrights, for some of their canoes were outfitted with sails and reportedly could carry up to 50 passengers. The Carib supported their economy by fishing and the cultivation of an unusually large variety of fruits. As might be expected in a society where military prowess was of paramount importance, the day-to-day operation of the family and village fell to the women. They tended the fields, reared the children, took care of the houses, and catered to the whims of the men.

The aboriginal population of the Caribbean islands, Arawak in the western Antilles and Carib in the east alike, declined precipitously with the onslaught of the European conquistadores. In the clash of the two cultures, Indian mores were practically eliminated within a century and a half. Indian biological traits also have long since been submerged by the overwhelming mass of Africans and Europeans. A few Caribs, or people who are predominantly Carib, live on a reserve on the island of Dominica. Elsewhere one finds an occasional trace of Carib stock virtually completing the inventory of the once widespread indigenous population.

The Indian political, economic, and social systems disintegrated before the passionate drive of the European to take full possession of the "new" land, people, and property. Plagues and a variety of illnesses accompanied the soldiers and sailors from disease-ridden Europe, and wreaked havoc among native people who had neither the natural immunity of the European nor local medicines to combat what were to them exotic maladies. Many Indians also perished after a short career as forced labor in placer-type mines and under various other conditions too debilitating for either their physical or psychological makeup. Then too, superior weapons and tactics from the militant countries of Europe must be credited with the decimation of many Indians and with the downfall or subjugation of native leaders.

Thus it appears that life for the average farmer or villager of the West Indies probably reached a pinnacle of physical, and perhaps economic and social, well-being more than 500 years ago. Since then —since that period during which food was plentiful and amazingly varied, when crowded housing and rural or urban slums did not exist, when virgin land was available almost for the taking, and trade based on the exchange of surplus goods was beginning to flourish—living conditions in the area have been on an irregular but generally unimpeded downward spiral in the face of nationalistic ambitions, a steadily swelling population, and ever greater competition for commercial gain.

The Slave Build-Up. As the Indian gradually faded out of the foreground of the Caribbean picture, and eventually even out of its background, the African became more and more in evidence. Introduced as slaves into the West Indies during the very early days of discovery, it was not until the latter half of the 17th century that black migrants forcibly brought from across the Atlantic began to swell the population. By that time sugar cane had become one of the most profitable crops in the Caribbean, and the planters' cry for more and more field hands was answered by the British Royal African Company and numerous other commercial firms which dealt in human merchandise.

Most of the African slaves were purchased by European traders from African slavers doing business along the west coast of Africa. The source of supply came from Angola northward and westward as far as Senegal, but the Congo and Nigeria apparently furnished the bulk of the slaves. The transferral of the hapless Africans to their new home in another hemisphere was usually accomplished under conditions which were at once gruesome from a humanitarian standpoint and inefficient commercially. Viewed in retrospect it is difficult to establish whether the high loss of life on board the slave ships was due primarily to ignorance of basic dietary and other health prerequisites, or to a callousness toward human suffering enhanced by the fact that the high margin of profit, or "mark-up," made it unnecessary to handle the merchandise with more than a modicum of care. There is no doubt, however, that the slave trade was a lucrative one. The market for sugar, and hence for plantation laborers, continued to grow. Since slave deaths regularly outnumbered births, traders had no difficulty in selling their cargo.

Most planters attempted to select the "right slave for the right job" on the basis of the physical characteristics of the individual man or woman on the block, but group characteristics also were taken into consideration. Slaves from one part of Africa, for example, had a reputation for their aggressiveness, whereas from other regions they were considered to be timid. Working conditions on the plantations varied, but it was a fairly common practice in many parts of the West Indies to grant the slaves sufficient time and land to grow some of their own provisions; to have allowed them to starve would hardly have proved a profitable business on the part of the planters.

The slaves were severely restricted in what they could and could not do, depending on the attitude and objective of their owners. In turn, some attempts were made on the part of officialdom to protect the slaves, for slaveowners also were subjected to certain restrictions, which varied with the nationality of the colony.

Slavery—Spanish Version. The institution of slavery played a far more dominant role in the New World than it did in contemporary Europe. Nonetheless the laws and customs of the Old World were carried by the civil servants across the Atlantic and formed the legal framework within which both slaves and slaver lived and worked. The slave laws of the Spanish West Indies provided, at least in principle, a measure of protection for the slave. He was considered to be a "person," not merely "property"—a most important distinction—and certain restrictions were therefore placed on the master's prerogatives. The master could actually lose his ownership rights in a slave as a result of proved maltreatment. A female slave, for example, who had been forced into prostitution by her owner could be compulsorily manumitted by the legal authorities.

Slaves could be freed for various reasons other than maltreatment by the owner. Owners not uncommonly freed their own half-breed offspring, and in the Spanish islands the custom of allowing slaves to purchase their own freedom was widespread. Under this practice, known as *coartación,* the slave usually paid over a long period of time for his freedom, but the master legally retained full control over him until the last payment had been made. (With the latter proviso, it is obvious that this early time-payment system was not the lineal ancestor of modern-day "travel now, pay later" credit plans.)

The law further stipulated that peaceful, freed slaves were not to be molested. Because of this legal protection, many runaway slaves from non-Spanish colonies fled to the then safe haven of Puerto Rico. Freed slaves early began to account for a large percentage of the population there and in other Spanish colonies. Cuba in 1774, for instance, contained a colored population estimated at 75,000; of these approximately 40 percent were free men and women.

Despite the fact that the manumitted slaves were "free under the law," they were at best second-class citizens. Regulations forbade the carrying of firearms by any Negro, whether free or slave. The free colored people were, among other restrictions, legally supposed to live under the supervision of a *patrón* and were forbidden to wear clothing considered unsuitable to their station in society. Relative, of course, to the severe restraints placed on most slaves, the "freed" slaves did have a large measure of independence.

To maintain a proper perspective, it is well to remember that even the white inhabitants of the Spanish colonies were under numerous restraints and restrictions. The royal court in Spain attempted to rule with a firm hand, and in many ways and at various periods of time this firmness reached down to the individual plantation owner as well as to the slave. Some scholars have suggested that if the laws in the Spanish colonies had been formulated by the creole landowners, as was the case to a certain extent in the British islands, the laws probably would have borne down even more heavily on the slaves. Thus, a relatively despotic government in Madrid attempted to hold the slaveowners in check and to provide some semblance of protection or at least consideration for the slaves.

As the sugar cane plantations increased in size and wealth, their owners gradually acquired a more effective voice in government. This slave-owning group became so powerful by the early part of the 19th century that its members were able successfully to resist, or modify, official policies. With this loosening of the reins from Madrid came a deterioration in the treatment of slaves; social conditions in the Spanish colonies began to resemble those in other sugar-based colonies.

Disregarding attempts of the Spanish colonial planters to embed the institution of slavery firmly and permanently into the mores of the region, the Spanish *Cortes* enacted legislation on the Fourth of July, 1870, designed to begin the process of abolishing slavery in Cuba and Puerto Rico. The legislation was not immediately effective, however, and was in fact more of a ploy in the gamesmanship of 19th-century international politics than it was a humanitarian effort.

British diplomats had huffed and puffed for many years to blow down the Spanish house of slavery, but aside from agreement in principle to eliminate the slave trade, little concrete progress had been made. By the late 1860's, however, Spain was facing crises at home and abroad, and was sorely in need of British support which, Britain had made abundantly clear, would not be forthcoming until some serious moves were made toward the abolition of slavery. At the same time, abolitionist sentiment was increasing in Spain and in the colonies.

In Cuba a bloody rebellion was underway; the rebels abolished slavery in principle but did little to enforce the measure for fear of alienating the sympathies of rich *criollo* planters. The United States, having just eliminated slavery at home, was bringing pressure on Spain to cede the island to the abolitionist Cuban rebels or, at least, to adopt a liberal reform program including an abolition measure.

The possibility was strong that the United States would soon give material support to the rebel cause, and perhaps even intervene more directly. Against these combined forces, the supporters of slavery retreated, but were still sufficiently powerful to water down the anti-slavery legislation and to delay its application until 1871 in Puerto Rico and 1872 in Cuba. Full abolition of slavery did not occur until 1873 in Puerto Rico—where slavery had but shallow roots—and 1886 in Cuba.

Slavery under the British. Traditions of representative government under the British political system have long included respect for the property rights of British citizens, and have allowed considerable freedom of action for the private entrepreneur. Slaves were considered by the colonial British to be a form of property; it therefore seemed only logical that the use of this property should be determined, as much as possible, by the property owner. This set of circumstances left the power of the slave owner over his slave virtually unlimited except by such laws and regulations as he and his fellow slave-owners deemed to be in their own best interests. The slave was merchandise to be bought and sold, mortgaged or inherited.

Although as early as the 1670's a few religious groups in the islands, such as the Quakers, were urging their members to treat slaves with kindness, laws aimed at protecting the slaves from mistreatment did not come about until the latter part of the 18th century, and probably only then because of active lobbying and agitation by organized humanitarian groups. Until that time, practically all of the regulations having to do with slaves were concerned with such topics as the pursuit, capture, and punishment of runaway slaves; prohibitions on the carrying of firearms or on assembly; penalties, often severe, for insulting or striking a white; and numerous restrictions aimed at controlling the slaves and thus maintaining public order.

Humanitarian interests gradually became more insistent, however, and laws were passed in island legislatures ameliorating the plight of the slaves. Once started, the notion that the slaves needed and deserved legal protection began to gather momentum. British agitators for the abolition of the slave trade and of the institution of slavery itself took the lead in the Caribbean. Thus slavery died an earlier death in the British colonies than in neighboring Spanish islands despite the earlier concern of Spanish laws for the well-being of the slaves.

In 1807 trade in slaves was abolished in the British Caribbean; and in 1833 the House of Commons passed the Emancipation Act (thus preceding Abraham Lincoln's Emancipation Proclamation by three decades). Although the not inconsiderable sum of £ 20 million was provided for the compensation of former slave owners, they considered the measure to be little short of expropriation since this figure amounted to about one half of the market value of the property.

The Act provided for a period of compulsory apprenticeship as an interim state between slavery and full emancipation. The ex-slave was required to remain at his job under his former master; the master was required to pay wages. The apprenticeship procedure soon proved unworkable and was abandoned in Jamaica in 1838 and elsewhere about the same time. In Antigua in 1834 the Moravian Brethren are given the credit for convincing the planters to grant full and immediate freedom to their slaves without the period of apprenticeship.

Life, Slavery, and the Pursuit of Happiness in the French, Dutch, and Danish Colonies.   In the French West Indies, unlike the British but like the Spanish islands, slavery was regulated by a legal code drawn up by the metropolitan government. Nevertheless, the early French laws governing slavery in French America fundamentally resembled those of the British West Indies. This interim position probably came about by virtue of laws prepared in consultation with local colonial authorities and strongly reflected the desires of West Indian slaveowners. At first, French law stressed the point that the slave might be "property," but he was also to be considered as a person. As such, he was to be baptized and given religious instruction; slave families were not to be broken when slaves were sold; and the master was responsible for furnishing adequate food, clothing, and shelter.

As more and more slaves were brought into the colonies, however, public and official concern for their well-being declined. Regulations safeguarding the slave as a person were permissively ignored or circumvented. Harsh regulations enforcing slave obedience became common, and, in general, the owner-slave relationship in the French West Indies became strikingly similar to those in other parts of the Caribbean. The French colonies, however, were swept along with the antislavery trend that picked up irresistible force in the 19th century, and in 1848 the French West Indian slaves were given their freedom.

The social conditions under which the slaves lived in both Dutch and Danish possessions were closely akin to those in other European colonies. The slaves were kept "in line" by the police-state methods common to the area and time; and as the ratio of Negro to white increased, the slave laws became more strict. As repression grew, so did the pressure for reform, and in the end the reformers triumphed. The slaves were freed in the Dutch West Indies in 1863 and in the Danish Caribbean in 1876.

5 *The Modern West Indians*

EMANCIPATION, though unquestionably the most outstanding single social advance ever accomplished in the Caribbean, by no means proved a cure-all. Indeed, not only did human suffering continue, but the economy of the islands took some steps backward.

Quo Vadis, Ex-Slave? Freedmen failed to receive the full rights of voting citizens. But then, few people, white or black, in the colonies were enfranchised. The various Acts of Emancipation did free the Negro from the legalized, and not infrequently brutal, discipline of the field gang. Some, of course, were forced by the sheer necessity of survival to continue working under the harshest of economic and social conditions, but many deserted the back-breaking labor in cane fields and other disagreeable chores to become squatters in outlying areas, especially the hill country.

So eager were many of the newly freed men to escape both site and sound of their former masters—despite the relative security that continued work on the old homestead offered—that they chose to gamble on their own ability to wrest a livelihood from the marginal or submarginal land that was available to them. Some fled to the backwoods because they were too lazy or too ill or too undernourished to withstand any more of the sunup-to-sundown drudgery so typical of the workaday routine on the plantations. Others fled because they were free to flee—as rational a reason as the force that impels a man to accept any challenge offered by his environment, such as climbing a mountain simply "because it's there." Some began to scratch out a miserable existence on the mountainsides or other deserted areas because they were afraid to stay with the former master, and others stayed because they were afraid to go. And who knows how many remained on the job at the familiar site simply because—for them—the management and pay were satisfactory?

The effect on agriculture of a shifting labor force was drastic. Since there were no large-scale schemes for the resettlement of freed slaves in the islands, subsistence farming on a strictly hand-to-mouth basis became widespread. There had evolved no moderately well-off farming class which could form the backbone of a stable society. The unsystematic movement which did result laid the groundwork for much of the land tenure pattern to be observed to this day—for example, hillsides dotted with tiny thatched huts and surrounded by tiny patches of farm lands.

To substitute for the dearth of farm hands following emancipation, some progressive planters turned to labor-saving devices. A steam plow introduced in Antigua replaced the Negro and his hoe; oxen-driven and horse-driven plows in other islands did likewise. Some plantations switched to cattle and sheep farming, thus requiring fewer workers. Probably the most widespread approach to the problem, however, was the attempt to replace the slaves with imported, paid laborers.

POPULATION GROWTH

Plantation owners and government officials brought workers from Spain, Portugal, Madeira, England, Ireland, India, China, and Africa. These newcomers, in many instances, were unable to produce as effectively as had the slaves. They were confronted with an environment far different from that which they had known in the "old country." Those from the middle latitudes had much to learn about tropical farming and, indeed, tropical living. One group of Englishmen, though perhaps not a typical one, was described by a contemporary observer as being "ill-selected, ill-conducted, ignorant, infirm, and most unsuccessful." * Nevertheless they came, and they

* *From The Historical Geography of St. Kitts and Nevis, The West Indies,* by Gordon C. Merrill, p. 90, quoting *The West Indies before and since Slave Emancipation* (London, 1854), by John Davy, p. 449.

continued to come. Some arrived in sponsored groups and others came individually; some came by first-class passage, and many by shoestring. On arrival, they were absorbed by both town and countryside.

In addition to growth in population by immigration, the so-called "natural increase" of the population of the West Indies has been one of the fastest of any region in the world. By 1963 there were estimated to be more than 19 million people scattered about the 91,200 square miles of the West Indies.* (See statistical appendices for island-by-island data on area and population.) And the end in accelerated population growth in the West Indies is not yet in sight. By 1975 the population in the region is expected to reach more than 27 million; and if the present rate continues, the not-too-distant turn of the century should find some 48 million people crowding the islands. Although the population of the Caribbean is expected to increase at a slower rate than most other parts of Latin America, the percentage gain far outruns that expected for any other major region of the world under the assumption of current fertility and continuous improvement in mortality (with the possible exception of South Asia).

The rate of population growth has varied considerably from island to island. The population of the British Islands has increased more slowly than has the population of Cuba or Puerto Rico. Trinidad, however, is an outstanding exception to this generalization because immigration there was extremely heavy. Trinidad's eleven-fold expansion between 1844 and 1960 has been, by far, the greatest in the Caribbean. Historically, the rate of population growth in each of the islands has been in direct response to both local and external influences, so that few valid generalizations can be made for the West Indies as a whole. Using Trinidad again as an example, we see that in the early days settlement was so limited that by 1783 there were fewer than 3,000 people in the island. By 1797, however, when the British took control, more liberal colonization measures had resulted in a rapid flow of immigrants, and the total population had risen to almost 20,000. In St. Kitts and Nevis, on the other hand,

* Including the Bahamas.

the population remained remarkably stable for more than two centuries, and only in the last two decades has there been a decided upturn. Barbados illustrates still another growth pattern; the population of this overcrowded island has not doubled within the last century.

In recent years, emigration has been the safety valve that has helped to keep the population pressure below the exploding point in Puerto Rico and, to a lesser degree, in Jamaica. Ready access to improved economic opportunities in the expanding labor market of mainland United States, unemployment or underemployment at home, and relatively cheap transportation have resulted in a rapidly increasing flow of Puerto Ricans to the north, particularly to New York City. The second migratory stream from the Caribbean was of more recent origin, in fact almost entirely a postwar phenomenon. British West Indians, particularly Jamaicans, have migrated to the United Kingdom for much the same reasons that Puerto Ricans have gone to New York: unsatisfactory employment conditions at home, job opportunities abroad, available transportation, and unrestricted entry into the United Kingdom until mid-1962, when Jamaica received its independence.

Many other modern, though less spectacular, migratory flows also indicate the economic pressure and lack of employment opportunities in the West Indies. Seasonal migration during crop seasons accounts for appreciable inflows and outflows of labor, providing temporary employment. Restrictions and regulations prevent any appreciable movements of a permanent nature, for each government seeks to preserve the maximum amount of national wealth and income for its own people. Understandably, clandestine emigration takes place both from island to island as well as to the nearby mainland. The recent influx of Cuban refugees to Florida illustrates a politico-economic rather than a purely economic motive for those on the move.

LURE OF THE CITY

As in most parts of the world, rural dwellers in the West Indies pour into the cities. Usually the larger the city, the faster they pour in. In fact, some of the smaller cities as well as villages and rural landscape have recently been losing population, relatively at least, if not actually. San Juan, Kingston, Havana, Port-au-Prince, Santo Domingo, and Port of Spain have all become metropolitan centers. San Juan serves to illustrate how the population of the large city outpaces that of the political entity in which it is located. In 1960 metropolitan San Juan, including Bayamón, Carolina, Cataño, and Guaynabo, had 589,104 people, or 25.1 percent of the entire population of Puerto Rico. In 1920 Bayamón, Carolina, Cataño, and Guaynabo were small, relatively unimportant settlements, certainly not a part of the San Juan cityscape. At that time San Juan only had 70,707 inhabitants, or 5.4 percent of the island's total population.*

The swelling of cities cannot be attributed to planning of any type nor to any specific development taking place in the West Indies. Rather, the influx of people has taxed and continues to tax urban facilities to the point that steps must be taken to provide low-cost housing facilities and otherwise curb the mushrooming of slum districts and their attendant evils.

The press, radio, movies, and now television all transmit to humble folks around the countryside the marvels of life in the big city. More directly, word-of-mouth tales of city life told by relatives, friends, or even chance acquaintances, sound like high adventure when related in a colorless village. So what is to prevent the ruralite or villager from setting out to seek a fortune in what appears to be greener pastures? Perhaps these restless people are holding to the tradition established many years before in Latin America when the Spanish conquistadores marched thousands of miles in search of the "fabulously wealthy" but elusive cities of Cibola. The difference between then and now may be no more than a matter of signposts. Cibola and its symbolic lure was always just over the horizon; today's route to glamor is a beaten one with inexpensive bus service.

The modern city is definitely not a mirage as was the Cibola of

---

* This method of computing San Juan's urban population in relation to that of Puerto Rico is not necessarily good statistical procedure, but from the standpoint of comparing the largest urban agglomeration at two dates, 40 years apart, it realistically presents the situation.

old. For many West Indians it is the source of a richer life in both
the cultural and commercial sense. Given limited job opportunities
at home in the rural area, a widespread system of land ownership
not far removed from feudalism, ever-increasing population pressure
on overworked land, few schools, and a lack of social mobility in a
rigid society, it is small wonder that potential riches of the city
beckon and the country folk respond. Against such a dull rural
backdrop, life in the city for many a newcomer is bearable and,
despite what may seem to some eyes to be pitiful and squalid conditions, represents an advance in living standards. The difficulties encountered in the city by rural migrants ignorant of the ways and
tempo of their new environment should not be glossed over nor
lightly dismissed. Nevertheless, the fact that they have broken with
a past full of disillusionment in favor of at least a chance for a better
life provides an incentive for continued effort. While many have
been trapped in miserable slums, others have merely used them as a
staging station en route to a more amenable life.

Today the cities of the Caribbean still contain appallingly large
slums, but change is the order of the day. On some islands improvements take place at near-revolutionary speed considering the job to
be done; elsewhere the pace progresses with irking lassitude because
of the competition for government funds. In Puerto Rico alone
nearly 100,000 modern dwelling units have been built since 1950,
zoning laws have effectively guided urban land use, an up-to-date
code of construction requirements has been established, and other
measures have quelled the expansion of existing slum areas. Only
within the last few years *El Fanguitos* (Little Mudholes), an un-
sightly agglomeration of shacks in San Juan, has given way to
pleasant housing developments. Those slums which remain are
gradually being eliminated by public housing and urban redevelopment programs. Attendant to this improvement, maximum effort is
being put into creating new jobs for both old and new residents
since even the cheapest of public housing cannot be afforded by the
unemployed. Unfortunately, progress along such redevelopment lines
has not been so spectacular in other parts of the Caribbean, but an

established trend is evident throughout the area; only the speed and magnitude differ.

Urban development and redevelopment in the Caribbean in recent years has drawn on the techniques developed in the most technologically advanced countries of the world, but the end result has not been a carbon copy of cities elsewhere. The architecture and general scheme of urban development have combined the local and the foreign. Many of the new buildings and development projects have a certain style and flair that is a reflection of the current renaissance of Latin America in general and of the Caribbean in particular—the genus is Latin American, the species Caribbean—with even more specialized variation from place to place within the Caribbean.

No claim is here made that Caribbean architecture has achieved a perfect blend of the physical and cultural environments of the area. There are, in fact, many discordant architectural structures, some left over from previous days and some just in the process of being built. But by and large, the architecture of the Caribbean increasingly reflects both the physical landscape and the particular experiences, past and present, of the local people. Much of it exudes an unfettered freshness that seems to suit the milieu quite well; it shows more concern for what is here now and what is to come in the future than for past glories.

The Primate City. As in most Latin American countries, *one* city has grown inordinately larger than others within the same country. This concept of a primate city, touched on above, shows up prominently in the West Indian distribution of urban population. In no other part of the world do we so consistently find the most populated city to be so many times larger than the secondary cities. This overwhelming dominance of primate cities is illustrated by Havana, with seven times as many people as the second Cuban city, and Port-au-Prince, with a population six times that of the second Haitian city. Santo Domingo in the Dominican Republic and San Juan in Puerto Rico each have almost four times as many people as the second metropolitan areas in their respective countries. By comparison New York City, despite its tremendous size, has only slightly more than double the population of the second American city.

Although the numerical superiority of these primate cities is more impressive in modern-day statistics, the tendency for this dominance is not a recent occurrence. In colonial times the key institutions of government and church were located in one city, the capital. Commercial enterprises, desiring to be near the source of power, clustered nearby, while transportation lines fanned out from them. Once the pattern was entrenched, it became increasingly more difficult for a secondary or tertiary city to meet the competition. Upon national independence, or with increased autonomy, the capital city remained the focus of political, commercial, and cultural affairs.

Bitterness occasionally develops between the citizens of the primate city and others in the country, the latter complaining that everything goes to or stays in the capital. Nevertheless, the fact that a primate city exists may well be justified. A country of limited resources might not be able to adequately support multiple concentrations of major institutions and their skilled professional personnel. Distribution of urban functions for the sole purpose of creating equilibrium would certainly make no sense. In addition, the concentration and close interrelationship found in the large city comprise the *raison d'etre* of many administrative functions, services, and amenities.

A primate city in the West Indies does not generally typify its country as a whole. In the very process of aggrandizement these cities have taken on a cosmopolitan appearance with a tempo and manner of living differing markedly from that of the country as a whole. In fact, the primate city may in some ways resemble comparably sized cities throughout the world and offer practically the same conveniences and services. Outside of the primate city, however, life goes on in a far different manner, not necessarily worse or better, but definitely lacking urban sophistication. It follows, then, that Santo Domingo or Kingston can by no means be considered as representative for the Dominican Republic or Jamaica.

CULTURAL MUSEUM

The people of the West Indies share many physical characteristics, have great similarities in their cultural backgrounds, and by and large are struggling with the same set of problems in the modern world. Nevertheless, the tapestry of their life is far from monochromatic; in fact, many of the colors are vibrantly different. In political theory governments and people alike must adhere to certain goals, but the approaches to them vary in the West Indies as much as in the world at large. Even in religion, a cultural aspect as basic as one can find, there is a wide spectrum of beliefs.

The majority of people in most of the islands are Roman Catholics; as exceptions the Bahamas, Barbados, St. Vincent, and Jamaica are predominantly Protestant. In Trinidad, Roman Catholics and Protestants balance out in number, but Hindus account for more than 20 percent of the population and Moslems for about 6 percent. Splinter groups are also active throughout the Caribbean. In Cuba and Haiti especially, but certainly not exclusively, many of the religious rites have strong African overtones, having obviously passed down from slavery and preslavery days. Voodooism, beneath its tourist veneer, still represents a serious carry-over of primitive, centuries-old superstitions.

Even in relation to ethnic or racial composition the West Indian scene presents a complicated picture. Cuba and Puerto Rico, according to the census reports, are more than three-fourths "white"; the Dominican Republic is listed as about one-fourth "white" and more than one-half "mixed"; most of the remainder of the islands are overwhelmingly Negroid, with a white population of less than 5 percent. Trinidad, as usual, is the nonconformist; about half its people are of African descent, a third of East Indian ethnic origin, and most of the remainder "mixed." The only other significant colony of east Indians in the West Indies (East-Indian West Indians, as it were) is in Jamaica, where they represent nearly one percent of the population.

Linguistically also, the islands give the impression of a potpourri.

It may come as no surprise that English is the most common language of the British West Indies, but the statement tells only part of the story. In the "British" islands of St. Lucia and Dominica, a French-derived patois is the mother tongue of most of the people; many of the residents of these two islands are able to speak only the patois, while others are bilingual. In the more truly English-speaking islands, there is a tremendous difference between the English spoken by the educated people (to many ears this is the most pleasing and only musical English spoken in the world) and the Creole variant used by the "man in the street." And even from British island to British island the variants may vary, each being a distinctive dialect.

French and French patois (called "Creole" in Haiti and "Patois" in the Lesser Antilles) are spoken in some of the British Windwards, as mentioned above, as well as in Haiti, Guadeloupe, and Martinique. Spanish, with only a few scattered exceptions, is the common tongue of Cuba and the Dominican Republic—that is, for about 55 percent of all the people in the West Indies. In Puerto Rico, basically a Spanish-speaking island, English is fast becoming a second tongue. Particularly the more highly educated people and those who have spent some time in "continental" United States can use English fluently. Nevertheless, less than a fourth of the Puerto Ricans can be characterized as truly bilingual. In the Netherlands Antilles, Dutch and Papiamento, the latter a patois evolved principally from Dutch and Spanish, are heard most frequently. But in addition English, French, and Spanish give the little islands, especially Aruba and Curaçao, a Tower of Babel effect, further suggested by the towering structures of the great oil refineries built here.

Lᴀᴛᴇ in the first half of last century an elementary school geography had the following to say about environment and crops in the West Indies:

> The West Indian islands are noted for the rich tropical produce with which, for two centuries, they have supplied the civilized world.
> The climate, tempered by the mountain air and sea breezes, is delightful during the greater part of the year; but, in autumn, hurricanes are sometimes destructive.
> The chief productions and exports are sugar, rum, molasses, coffee, tobacco, allspice, oranges, pineapples, and other luscious fruits. . . .*

Without sinking into the mires of environmental determinism, one can see that the basic production pattern of the archipelago is now substantially what it was 116 years ago. Quite naturally a number of embellishments have been added to the scene, and not a few evils have crept in to throw such a nice-sounding economy off balance. One cannot expect the sequence of economic, cultural, and political action taking place on the islands to remain static. If nothing else, variations in the price of sugar can make or break fiscal regimes and spell prosperity or poverty to the mass of population on any given island or group of islands.

Temperate-Tropical Balance. The underlying structure of West Indian economy can in great part be traced to the attraction of tropical commodities to a temperate people. In centuries gone by Europeans, far more advanced technically than the Antillean aborigines, were able to establish a highly profitable flow of goods to their shores. Once the worth of sugar and other tropical crops in European

---

* Morse's *School Geography,* Harper and Brothers, New York, 1848.

markets had been ascertained, a routine of plantation culture
evolved, though in part by trial and error. Slowly the know-how of
one group in one area would filter to other groups in other areas.
Decimation of native inhabitants and the active, large-scale slave
trade to provide labor attest the deadly seriousness of this expansive
transatlantic venture with its aura of wealth and gracious living for
the successful entrepreneur.

The high regard in which the West Indian islands and their
exotic crops were held by Europeans is admirably illustrated by an
oft-told experience of Benjamin Franklin during his days as a diplo-
mat in Western Europe. In the late 18th century during the negotiations that led to the Treaty of Paris, he actually had to press the
British to accept Canada rather than the sugar-producing island of
Guadeloupe as the price for ending the war with France.

So deep-rooted was the plantation system over the islands that the
traditions still persist in many aspects. One must note that throughout the West Indies the big enterprise—modern-day version of the
plantation—is one of the few ways that a small nation can remain
economically viable or that a dependency can, to a degree at least,
stand on its own feet. Americans may, of course, look to a similar
evolution of the Deep South of their own country to see the rem-
nants of an economic pattern formerly dependent upon the plantation concept.

The flow of tropical commodities from the West Indies to Europe
continues east-northeastward across the Atlantic, but trade channels
have also diverged to send sugar, coffee, bananas and other items to
temperate lands in widespread directions. In turn, the market in the
West Indies for commodities from temperate lands has increased
considerably since the heyday of colonial plantations, resulting in a
two-way rather than primarily a one-way trade. Thus, European
countries that formerly sponsored the movement now more accu-
rately qualify as participants, or trading partners. While the same
type of tropical-temperate interchange goes on in other parts of the
world, it is in Caribbean waters that one discerns so easily the pattern in its full evolutionary sequence.

The most recent development involving the supplementary relationship of exchange between tropical West Indies and temperate Europe can be read into Communists' economic planning for Cuba. Sugar cane is to be grown expressly for the Soviet Union and its satellites, regardless of geographic location or previously established channels of trade (see more complete discussion in Chapter 7).

Basis for an Economy. At the outset any West Indian economy must necessarily be gauged by agricultural production. Minerals, forestry, manufacturing, commerce, fishing, and tourism, while not to be discounted as sources of livelihood and revenue, are severely limited in the amount of long-term basic support they can contribute in sustaining a population of nearly 22 million—and more to come. Thus, the critical factor of the West Indian environment is that part which favors plant growth.

Relief, soil, water supply, and temperatures appear in combinations favorable to the growth of a great variety of tropical and subtropical crops. Some areas on the West Indian islands cannot be exceeded for productivity, such as Cuba's fertile red clay soils accounting for some of the highest sugar yields per acre in the world, or Haiti's superb hilly tracts permitting growth of prize-winning aromatic coffee beans. Yet three of these basic resources in turn suffer from environmental limitations which do not meet the eye in any inventory of resources or listing of natural advantages: low ratio of level to mountainous terrain, deficient soils, and low effectiveness of precipitation.

It has already been stated that the West Indies may be realistically described as a partially submerged range of mountains. The type of sharp and rugged relief on most islands automatically precludes a high proportion of the surface as agriculturally productive. Even those level or relatively level areas may have soils unsuited to cultivation, such as the swampy areas along the north and south coasts of Cuba and the east and west coasts of Trinidad. Many areas, though credited as productive, have poor soils due to deficiencies in plant nutrients, heavy erosion, stoniness, or other shortcomings. For example, the U.S. Department of Agriculture in its 1942 Soil

Survey of Puerto Rico rates only one-sixth of the arable land of the island as having top-quality soil.

The West Indies lie in the wet, not dry, tropics. Some of the rainfall statistics sound impressive; Jamaica, for example, has an average island-wide fall exceeding 75 inches and one spot registering 222 inches per year. Yet a closer analysis of the precipitation and its effectiveness reveals a water shortage in places. In some areas this shortage limits the type or quality of crop; in others, cultivation is prevented altogether. Leeward slopes, creating rain shadows; high temperatures, accelerating the rate of evaporation; and porous soils, incapable of holding moisture well, combine to render rainfall less meaningful for vegetative growth. Some lee areas of mountainous islands actually exhibit the characteristics of semi-arid lands with cactus-like plants. If irrigation is possible, it is only part of the answer because of the additional cost and energy required to produce crops where the margin of profit is already low.

Only the high sun offers a never varying advantage to the West Indian agricultural regime. The growing season everywhere runs a full year, and warm sunshine pervades all parts of all islands.

Since agricultural production generally serves as the mainstay of West Indian islands, percentage of arable land needs to be taken into account to obtain a more realistic picture of the man-land ratio. Densities per square mile should be reviewed carefully in relation to arable land. For example, one finds that Haiti's reported 406 persons per square mile must for the most part rely on 13.7 percent of the country's area for their sustenance. The density per square mile of arable land is thereby boosted to 2,969 persons. Next, apply the rate of population growth to a figure like this and project what the pressure of population is going to be in 1974, 1984, and so on. Thus, development of industries other than agriculture has double worth since any success in such projects reduces the pressure on the limited amount of productive land.

Patchwork of Local Economies. Economic patterns vary markedly from island to island throughout the West Indian archipelago. Differences in the physical base account for some deviation from a norm; relief, rainfall, and soil, as has been pointed out, have their own mosaic quality. Beyond this diversity, the size of any given island puts a stamp on its economic capabilities and potential. Cuba is 10 times the size of Jamaica; Jamaica is 10 times the size of Martinique; and, in turn, Martinique is nearly 10 times the size of Montserrat. What opportunities do the smaller islands have to establish in any realistic or practical measure an economy that may be regarded as self-sufficient? At best a specialty crop or product is exported to bring in enough revenue to allow importation of the necessities of life for the inhabitants and perhaps an occasional luxury item. Sugar, on little islands and big islands alike, constitutes the cash crop. Coffee, bananas, tobacco, cacao, coconuts, and citrus fruits in irregularly scattered fashion also contribute to a more sophisticated type of economy. On a smaller scale some of the islands indulge in unusual crops or products as specialties. Two interesting examples are arrowroot in St. Vincent and angustora bitters in Trinidad.

Lacking the means of producing cash crops, islanders can do little more than try to eke out a subsistence, aided by some form of subsidy from the metropole or a country equipped to give grants in aid.

Britain, France, the Netherlands, United States, Denmark, Spain, and, very recently, the Soviet Union, all have had a hand in molding the diverse economies in the West Indies. Certain relationships perforce evolved between a developing West Indian island and the maritime nation controlling its destiny through the colonial period. That the bits of land changed hands also brought about overlapping types of cultures and ways of engaging in economic activities. For example, there are French-speaking pockets on British islands harking back to the raiding parties of colonial days. In the Dominican Republic and Haiti many Spanish and French techniques linger. With the waning of direct European influence in the Caribbean during the last century and a half the impact of the nearby and fast-growing United States became increasingly felt. Investments, stimulation of trade, and tourist interest by Americans have brought the islands into close proximity to the American scene socio-economically as well as geographically. With few exceptions the newer installations on most islands are of an American type. In Haiti it is interesting to note that for important transactions dollars flow more freely than does the domestic *gourde* (equal to $0.20) as a medium of exchange. The Soviet influence in Cuba has sharply turned the *way* of doing things to a Marxist pattern, but much time would be required to eradicate the Spanish and American appearance of the cultural landscape.

The Bind of Land Tenure. The pattern of ownership of agricultural land serves as a key to understanding the economy of any state, especially in Latin America, where it has long imperiled effective development of most agrarian areas. The West Indian islands have proved to be no exception. Here the history of land tenure has generally fallen into one of two unfortunate but apparently unavoidable patterns:

(1) Ownership of large holdings by a select few, known as *latifundia,* on which the tenants have little or no margin above mere survival for themselves and their families; and

(2) Ownership by the tenant, but of holdings so small that he is again hard pressed to survive.

Large holdings are modern counterparts of colonial plantations. After the abolition of slavery in the 19th century, landowners faced the necessity of wholesale reorganization in their method of operation. Wage workers and tenants replaced slaves, but their flexibility raised difficulties to be resolved. Competition increased as tropical regions in other parts of the world were opened up and developed. Especially pertinent to the sugar growers was beet-sugar competition from Europe itself, and later from the United States. Too, mechanization and other innovations in production were forced on West Indian planters by a world technically on the move. Gone were the days of lush living when any plantation flourished by producing, however inefficiently, for a growing market.

In material goods the wage earners and tenants were little if any better off than their bonded predecessors. Slaves at least did not have to worry about slack seasons and unemployment. On the other hand, circulation of workers from one point of an island to another and among islands as well as the great migration to cities testifies to

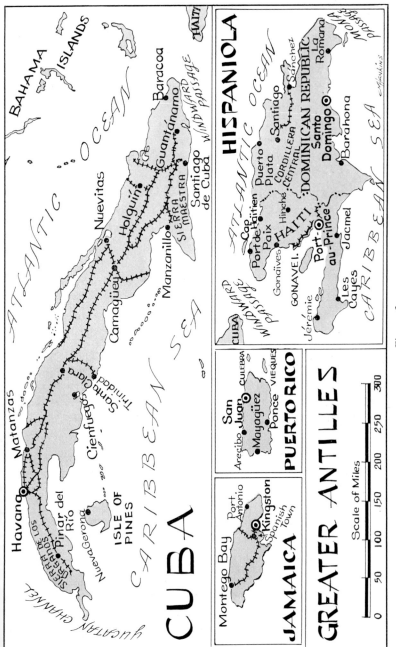

Figure 2

Figure 3

Figure 4

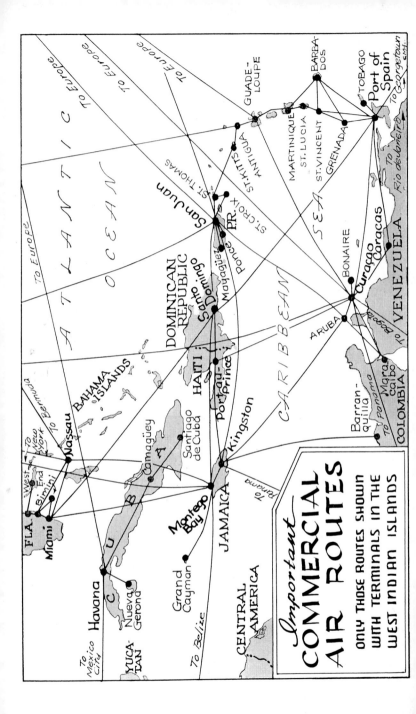

the glorious appeal of seeking opportunities—limited though they be—in a free society.

Under conditions of a stable population small landholders might have a chance to adjust to self-sufficient cultivation with some reliance on a cash crop. But a relentlessly increasing population wreaks havoc on this type of social system. While the resource base of an island can without question be enriched and expanded, it cannot approach infinity to match mankind's well-demonstrated fertility.

The economic forces which favor small holdings for the most part work against profitable commercial farming. The growing of sugar cane especially requires large fields capable of mechanized tending and large mills to insure large-scale savings in grinding. Fortunately, some valuable crops lend themselves better to small-scale operators, as exemplified by the individual banana growers on Jamaica and some of the Lesser Antilles. Even here, however, big business enters the picture; a single mercantile firm collects the bunches for export to a proven market in Europe.

A favorite political gambit in the West Indies (as in many other parts of the world) is the framing of grandiose plans to divide large landholdings into small ones. In theory at least, such reforms point the way to long overdue social justice and imply improvement and stability in the economic system. Over the years virtually every West Indian island has experienced steps toward these measures. In many instances, however, the plans, though officially sanctioned, lagged long before being realized, if indeed they ever were realized. The "Five-Hundred Acre Law" enacted in Puerto Rico in 1900 made it illegal for a corporation to own or control more than 500 acres. Nevertheless, powerful interests continued for decade after decade to operate plantations of great size, as much as 100 times the maximum legal limit. Recent agrarian reform in Cuba has shattered large estates, but in true Communist fashion the state rather than individuals reap the benefits. Maximum sizes of farms are being reduced as the confiscation of land continues and more co-operative farms go into operation.

Under any circumstance the cutting up of large holdings, admirable though the gesture be, does not necessarily insure any group an improved standard of living or otherwise upgrade the economy. Political turmoil and the foundering of governmental regimes up and down the archipelago reflect the land-tenure bind, for here is a matter of widespread interest over which emotion and sentiment as well as cold economic logic reigns.

The Case for Industrialization. Every government in the West Indies strives to industrialize as a means to better the economy of its people. Some try harder than others, and some are meeting with more success than others. Probably none of the political entities, whether independent or associated with metropole states (mother countries), has illusions of becoming an industrial power. Nonetheless, the rigors of hard pressed economies force steps in this direction despite the handicaps posed by physical barriers and economic immaturity.

At the outset, heavy manufacturing must be stricken from any list as an industrial potential in the West Indies. Minerals in sufficient supply or the right combination would at best allow only spotty development. Mineral industries which do exist generally involve extraction or processing—for example, exploitation of bauxite in Jamaica and petroleum refining in Trinidad. Lack of capital, inadequate technical training, and absence of a substantial market only compound the physical shortcomings.

Certain industries do lend themselves to successful development if geared to the existing resources and the social capabilities and complexes of the inhabitants. They may be divided into two general types: (1) processing of agricultural commodities, and (2) fabrication of light and medium goods for the home or regional markets. Also attractive to island entrepreneurs, but somewhat oblique to the above categories, is the utilization of inexpensive labor to manufacture high-value products using inconsequential amounts of raw materials. Quality textiles or parts for electronic equipment best illustrate the type.

Among the products resulting from the processing of agricultural crops, sugar, rum, and molasses lead the field on most islands by a wide margin. Preparation of harvested coffee beans, cacao pods, and tobacco leaves likewise stands high in specific areas. The canning of pineapples on Guadeloupe and Martinique represents a highly specialized agricultural industry suitable to the environment and responding to a favorable market in the metropole of these two islands.

Crisscross Commerce. The exports of Cuba, Haiti, the Dominican Republic, and most of the British islands relate directly to the agricultural products processed—50 percent or more, depending upon the leading crop. In Trinidad and Tobago and the Netherlands Antilles petroleum products comprise the preponderant export, about 75 and 95 percent respectively. As an exception, Puerto Rico is able to account for nearly three quarters of its exports by manufactured goods and handicrafts which incorporate traditional skills of the population for needlework and other of the textile arts.

Imports conform to no set pattern. Items frequently appearing on the lists of incoming goods include miscellaneous food products, flour, textiles and fabrics, machinery, chemicals, fertilizers, and motor vehicles. Some of the archipelago's leading export items also need to be imported to certain of the other islands, such as petroleum products and even sugar.

The United States generally plays a dominant role as the country of origin of West Indian imports and destination of exports other than in the British and French islands. However, in Jamaica, the Bahamas, British Virgin Islands, and Cayman Islands, trade with Britain is exceeded by that with the United States. Canada, other West Indian islands, and countries of Western Europe also figure prominently as trading partners. Since 1959 the heavy Cuban-United States axis of trade has been re-oriented across the Atlantic to the Soviet Union and countries of Eastern Europe.

A certain proportion of the commodities processed locally goes no farther than the domestic market, such as cigarettes and a number of food and beverage products. In addition, numerous other products are manufactured for local consumption, comprising, in fact, the bulk of non-complex goods needed in large quantities: textiles, leather goods, simple metal wares, construction items, and some chemicals. A cement factory has often represented the initial step of a government's endeavors to diversify and expand the local economy. Such enterprises are thought to touch off a chain reaction which augurs well in raising standards: (1) provision of needed items at less cost, (2) reduction of imports, (3) additional employment, and (4) opening up opportunities for associated industries and activities, including servicing and by-products. Puerto Rico especially has benefited from this type of economic up-grading.

In spite of the apparently simple and obvious economic philosophy just expounded, industrial improvement is a long, slow, uphill pull. In most of the islands little capital is to be found with which to start large-scale commercial enterprises and build factories. The average islander must spend most if not all of his productive energies for food, clothing, and shelter. A savings account is usually beyond his ken. In Haiti the rural housewife spends a whole day at the market selling a basket of wretched onions. How can a society of these financial dimensions come up with the surplus for capital investment?

Fun in the Sun. Pleasure-seeking visitors bring enough revenue to the West Indies for tourism to be considered a leading economic activity or even an "industry." Beyond giving employment to thousands of islanders, the high influx of tourist dollars stimulates the economy in many other ways and adds to the importance and prestige of capital cities and resort centers. In 1962 the Caribbean islands were left $160 million richer by American visitors. Even so, this impressive figure represented a decrease from previous years when Havana was a magnet of attraction to enormous numbers of United States citizens.

Tourist attractions of the West Indian archipelago are multiple and self-generating as specific places and activities become known. Location relatively near the populous eastern seaboard of the United States serves as an initial advantage. Though Europe still far outweighs the West Indies as the ultimate in foreign travel for Americans, the latter nonetheless holds special merit to large numbers who treasure days in a smiling, salubrious climate. A summer as well as a winter "season" now grace the West Indian travel folder and tariff cycle. Natural advantages also extend to stark mountainous scenery, exotic tropical vegetation, and unlimited miles of inviting beaches. The insular nature of the region also intrigues Americans, for they like to hop from island to island and to be able to travel across the tiny "continents" in a matter of a fraction of a day or in some places even in minutes. They find the contrast of these fractured land forms with their own broad homeland intriguing, overwhelming.

History and culture of the islands appeal to the average tourist only superficially. The legend of Bluebeard or stirring accounts of buccaneer depredations may be of passing interest, or it may strike his fancy to see a voodoo ceremony (specially arranged) or take in "picturesque villages" from a fast-moving vehicle. Much more to his liking are apt to be the wide varieties of imported goods purchasable at custom-free ports, native handicraft items in gift shops, and the bar on the cruise ship. The luxury hotel acts as the greatest boon to tourism in this tropical setting, especially favoring the airborne traveler who, to pay any kind of a visit to the spot of his choice, must alight and at least stay overnight. Here in air-conditioned comfort he can escape even the wafting breezes of the Trade Winds. Irrespective of tourist motives, however, the dollars pour into the islands and fashion certain segments of the economy.

Without question, Havana before the day of Castro was the celestial city of Caribbean tourism. Convenient to Miami and Key West and not a long flight from New York, it offered the foreign touch in spectacular proportions—a shiny tropical city ornate with Spanish architecture, wide boulevards, and historical monuments, not to mention opportunity to make expenses at the race track and to bask on the white sand at nearby Varadero beach.

Many places other than Havana have of course sparkled on the travel agent's prospectus. Now that Cuba is off limits to the Caribbean tourist several other centers have accelerated in prominence. Montego Bay, a sleepy little settlement on the north coast of Jamaica as late as the early 1950's, now vies with Miami Beach and Cannes as a fashionable watering place. Nassau, almost an extension of Florida's golden east coast playground, receives on the order of $30 million per year from visitors. Ever greater numbers of luxury hotels plus attractive airline rates and complimentary rum drinks in the airport are making San Juan a popular center. In a recent year 1.6 million people moved in and out of Puerto Rico, a substantial number of them tourists. Santo Domingo and Port-au-Prince as capitals have likewise sought tourist trade by erecting enticing hostelries. In addition to these big, brassy centers the islands are filled with small centers and out-of-the-way spots intriguing as travel experiences or for sports.

Tourism in the West Indies also brings problems. Economies, especially on the smaller islands and in small communities, may be seriously disrupted by "windfall" spending of tourists, which lead local inhabitants to be discontent with the usual dull routine of their life. A tourist type of prosperity is not necessarily stable, for travel patterns change and at any time a political crisis can completely disorganize the best of travel plans. Haiti and the Dominican Republic have found it impossible to keep their hotels full to the tune of yelling mobs and gunfire.

Fragmented Transportation Net. In the West Indies as elsewhere in the world the economy has developed in about the same proportion as the transportation facilities. A fragmented sovereignty pattern over the Caribbean, however, has in turn fragmented lines of transportation. First steamship lines, then commercial air routes, tied the area in with Europe, North America, and South America (see Figure 5). Interisland service was incidental to these long-distance routes. Even now, more likely than not, to go from island "A" to island "B" one must catch a plane which originates at a large terminal such as New York, Miami, or London. Only a few interisland routes developed, these usually serving airports of like sovereignty: San Juan to Charlotte Amalie (St. Thomas), Port of Spain to Scarborough (Tobago), Havana to Nueva Gerona (Isle of Pines), and in the Bahamas. Only Cuba and Hispaniola have sufficient area to justify air route structures of any complexity within their confines. Small ships, including the sailing variety, also carry on local services among neighboring islands and along the coasts of the larger islands.

Sovereignty explains the lack of any sort of transportation network. Community of interest among the different states and colonial groups never reached an intensity which would require traffic of any significance. The greatest ties were with temperate areas with which the tropical islands could benefit by exchange of goods, particularly the United States, and between dependency and metropole.

In the 1950's a project was envisioned whereby the Pan American highway would be supplemented by a road extending through the islands. Ferry service would enable motorists to cover the water gaps. Had the venture materialized it would have been the first instance of regular water connections across Windward Passage, Mona Passage, and other straits which long have served as moats around political entities within the Caribbean.

In contrast to the lack of a unified regional transportation system, each island has facilities which to some degree at least take care of its own requirements. The nature of these individual insular patterns varies according to the coastal configuration and terrain. The facilities on the smaller islands may be quite primitive. On Hispaniola two independent patterns developed bearing little direct relationship one to the other.

Other than the longitudinal system of Cuba, no island has a railroad net worthy of the term. The Dominican Republic, Jamaica, and Trinidad each have short stretches of track connecting a few important centers. Haiti's 77 miles of trackage running north from the Port-au-Prince area has largely fallen into disuse, while Puerto Rico's coastal railroad circling most of the island has been completely abandoned. In addition to public railroads many miles of private lines throughout the West Indies have been constructed to haul sugar cane to the mill. About 7,500 miles of such industrial railways facilitate the Cuban sugar harvest, though obsolete equipment is taking its toll.

Roads are by far the most common type of transportation on the various islands. Although standards of living preclude large numbers of private automobiles except around some of the more important cities, buses run just about everywhere.

With but few exceptions, roads connect the larger cities of each island with the capital and with each other. It may be fairly said that in comparison to highway densities in the United States they form sparse networks. While these major roads are usually paved or have all-weather surfaces, many of the secondary roads in outlying areas become impassable during the rainy season. In Haiti in particular, road conditions in places may be questionable and long-distance intercity bus travel a gruesome experience.

The lack of a cohesive transportation net is yet another expression of the heterogeneous make-up of the Caribbean islands. It remains to look at each of the individual political entities and examine those traits characteristic of the archipelago unit by unit. In that way it is hoped that both the whole and the pieces will mesh to give a clearer picture of the West Indian scene.

Cuba

Tʜᴇ island of Cuba accounts for slightly less than one-half the land surface of the entire Antillean chain. Puerto Rico, diminutive by comparison, would fit into Cuba nearly 13 times. To travel the 730 miles from the eastern to the western extremity of the island would be equivalent to going from Washington, D.C., to St. Louis. Yet despite this relatively impressive bulk Cuba over the years has never dominated the West Indian scene in relation to its size. Scan pages of history and island names like Martinique, Barbados, and Jamaica will more than hold their own. Scan the literature, and a more romantic atmosphere exudes from Port of Spain, Pétionville, or Ocho Rios than from almost any spot in Cuba other than Havana and its fancy beach resorts. Only in the harshly realistic investment world and by a colossal production of sugar cane has Cuba seemed to overshadow the remainder of the archipelago.

Since 1959 the Revolution in Cuba has brought the island into the political limelight. Most writings on the subject—whether careful analyses or quickly pulled-together exposés on the treachery of Fidel Castro to his own people—accentuate political, historical, economic, and social aspects of Cuba's dilemma. A minimum amount of attention is given to geographic factors and their impact. It may be worthwhile in the next few pages to remark on those features of Cuba's environmental base which may have a bearing on the post-1959 country.

A Bountiful Nature. An environment rich in agricultural potentialities and favorable to many industrial pursuits gives Cuba a margin of natural wealth capable of partially sustaining the economic wastes of revolution and mismanagement by the Castro regime. It has been so in the past, and it is so now. Extensive areas of arable land favored by an optimum climate for numerous crops have never been under severe economic pressure to support the population—the reverse of the situation in many other Caribbean areas. Although the need to grind out a bare living by subsistence farming has long plagued the Cuban people, this handicap comes largely from nongeographic causes. Whether or not those blue-printing the 1959 Revolution deliberately took into account the advantage of an economic margin in their program is a moot question; the fact that it facilitated the movement is beyond question.

The latest available official statistics list nearly 80 percent of the total land surface as farmland. However, of the 22.5 million acres thus classified only about 4.9 million, or 22 percent, were actually under cultivation. Much of the remaining so-called arable land was held fallow, devoted to raising of livestock, or otherwise uncultivated in response to the demand for or restriction against additional sugar cane acreage. There appears to be no index of what the maximum agricultural production might be.

One of the most remarkable aspects of the Cuban landscape is the consistency of favorable conditions throughout the island. Three-fifths of the area is either relatively flat or undulating, while much of the mountainous land supports or could support some form of agricultural activity. Fertile soils, although varied in type, extend to all sections of the country other than rugged or marshy areas. Except in higher elevations the climate remains moderate and stable throughout the year. The over-all annual rainfall of 55 inches fluctuates both from place to place and from year to year, but seldom to the extent that crop damage is widespread. The only exception to this benign physical environment lies in the occasional hurricane which may sweep across the island.

Other geographic factors, too, facilitate an agricultural economy on Cuba. A long, narrow shape plus low relief and adequate harbors affords easy access to the sea; only one small area in the southeastern part lies more than 40 miles from the closest coastline. Further, the island is rimmed by a succession of pouch-shaped harbors. The same attenuated shape has likewise simplified land transportation by permitting the construction of longitudinal rail and highway systems, all parts of Cuba being relatively near these arterial trunk routes. Finally, the spaced distribution of mountainous areas means a minimum of barrier effect. Few areas of productive significance are sealed off or open only through strategic mountain passes. Perhaps the only exception of consequence is the Sierra Maestra range, which limits contact with the extreme southern coast. This same mountainous area, largest and most isolated in Cuba, has served as a spawning ground for revolutions. Here the present political leaders of the country began their onslaughts against the Batista government and consolidated their gains in the years immediately prior to taking over in Havana.

It is of more than passing interest to compare Cuba with Java, in some ways an eastern world counterpart. Java (including Madura) with its 51,032 square miles is only one-seventh larger than Cuba (including the Isle of Pines) with 44,218 square miles. Yet the 63,060,000 people living in Java outnumber the 7,203,000 living in Cuba by a ratio of about nine to one. Parts of Java have a density of population exceeding 1,500 per square mile. Both islands have roughly comparable areas of lowlands. The fertile volcanic soil constituting the agricultural base of Java's 19.4 million arable acres matches rather well the 22.4 million acres of principally limestone soil in Cuba.

One may speculate how well any Cuban economy, or political system, might stand up under a population pressure such as presently experienced by the Javanese. Has an abundant nature, with a margin for mistakes and experiments, not been at least partly responsible for the present government in Cuba?

Sugar Economy. Sugar cane in Cuba represents a classic example of a one-crop economy. It normally occupies one-half or more of all cultivated land on the island, requires nearly one-fourth of the labor force, and accounts for about four-fifths of the exports. The economics of Cuba truly revolves around this crop. Success of the crop has long served as an index to purchasing power, capital for investment, and general well-being among the inhabitants. Regardless of political control over the island here is an economic regime difficult indeed to remold other than ideologically.

In good years Cuba has produced 20 percent or more of the world's sugar cane. Actually, amounts of unrefined sugar may be tremendous. In 1957 the record bumper crop of more than 7 million tons would have furnished each person in the United States with approximately one-fourth of a pound of sugar every day for a year. Since the 1959 Revolution, production has slumped considerably, and by 1963 the harvest amounted to roughly 3.8 million tons.

The excellence of conditions for growing sugar was appreciated by Spanish colonists as early as the 16th century, though plantings were limited. Not until fairly late in the 18th century did the crop attain a predominate position in the national economy. Once technical processes were improved and markets created, production gained rapidly. The United States figured prominently in this meteoric rise, from both the investment and marketing standpoints. In fact, sugar was the magnet attracting close U.S. attention to Cuba at the turn of last century when Spanish control was being shaken off. With the phasing out of the American west for pioneer development investors eagerly turned to other areas for their bonanza, Cuban sugar lands among them. From then until 1959 the island's entire sugar industry remained closely integrated with the American economy.

Much evidence has been gathered to illustrate the shortcomings of a one-crop economy in Cuba. Critics of the system point out the advantages of diversification. The government from time to time has attempted to program or otherwise encourage an economy less dependent upon the sugar crop. Unfortunately the time never seemed right for remedial measures. When sugar prices were high, times were good and any incentive to diversify was lacking, or at least weakened. Then when prices plummeted downward, the whole island fell on hard times and any substantial means to diversify was lacking. The U.S. aid program in Cuba during the 1950's was directed in large part toward countering this imbalance.

Superficially, the case against Cuba's traditional and highly developed sugar economy appears impressive. Many of the disadvantages stand out clearly. The large labor force harvesting the crop and hauling it to the mill worked only from 4 to 6 months of the year. Thus, a great army of workers were hard pressed to find employment during the other months, many remaining idle. (Now, ironically, there appears to be a labor shortage.) Seeds of discontent are sown in any economic system with unemployment of such magnitude. An equally obvious handicap in the system rests in the lack of any control over price. Cubans prior to the Revolution sold their sugar in relation to the prevailing world market. In the 1920's sugar brought the unbelievably low price of .057 cents per pound, or $12.75 per long ton. Shortly before, only 57 pounds of sugar sold for more than this amount! Other evils of the system involved the ownership of land, high capital investment, and other aspects of big business which funneled more and more wealth into fewer and fewer hands.

A diversification program, if properly executed, could undoubtedly have gone a long way toward balancing the Cuban economy. Agriculturists could then have automatically hedged on world prices to insure importation of more commodities for domestic use. National industries other than sugar milling would have smoothed out the labor demand. A greater proportion of Cubans would have participated in entrepreneurial activities. Why, then, were diversification efforts so ineffective? The taste of prosperity during good years, and a chance for profit—the gambling urge—proved to be incentives powerful enough not only to continue dependence on sugar, but encouraged plunging ahead with production at every opportunity. Wheat farmers of Kansas and growers of early vegetables on our Atlantic coastal plains have similar attitudes; they do not diversify.

When the Castro government came into power, the announced policy depreciated sugar as the all-important crop. Rather, the national economy with diminished interest in sugar could direct investment and planning efforts toward diversification, especially industrialization. However, when the Soviets came more prominently into the picture, orders from Moscow rescinded any steps in this direction, and the demand was made that Cuba be a producer and supplier of sugar. The Soviets further made the provision that aid would be continued only under such terms. In face of this pressure Castro announced that industrialization would not be stepped up to the degree which was originally planned.

Ideally, one could reason that Cuba is an opulent producer of cane, and as such has a potential market of unlimited proportions in the U.S.S.R. and Eastern Europe with their heavy concentrations of industrial population. The question nonetheless remains open: Does the Soviet bloc really have need for millions of tons of sugar? Sugar beet production at hand, plus the long haul of the cane from the West Indies to Bloc ports, would suggest that the arrangement is somewhat less than perfect. Further complicating the situation, Bloc sugar quotas have not been met.

It is ironic and perhaps significant that Soviet Bloc technical advisors for Cuban agricultural methods, who have replaced those from the United States, come from areas where agricultural programs are failing to meet the necessary production standards. Also the high mid-latitudes of a continental climate makes a poor training ground for specialists in tropical agriculture.

Other Agricultural Activities. Despite the emphasis on sugar many other crops have been produced, and some attention is given to animal industries. Tobacco, although a poor second to sugar, is traditional to Cuban economy. Havana cigars earned an international reputation. More recently, production has gone into the manufacture of domestic cigars and cigarettes. A third commercial crop, coffee, likewise declined other than for the home market.

Rich soil and optimum climatic conditions so conducive to high sugar yields favor many cereal, root, and fruit crops. In fact, most agricultural regions would be a horticulturist's dream. The new government has given some support to production of henequen and cotton as fiber crops for local industries.

The relatively low population density permits large areas of pasture lands to be given over to livestock. Cattle for beef, for dairying, and as draft animals receive the most attention. In fact, before 1959 meat and dairy products together constituted the highest-ranking agricultural industry after sugar.

Industry. Cuba does not have the potential to specialize in heavy industry other than by subsidy or artificial stimulation. Lack of mineral fuels and water power, either developed or undeveloped, discourages most complex manufacturing activities. Furthermore, the population does not have the training necessary for turning the intricate wheels of industry.

Industrial pursuits are largely limited to the processing of agricultural products, especially the milling of sugar. Meat-packing, tanning of hides, manufacturing of cigars and cigarettes, and coffee roasting typify other industries, well justified in the face of a domestic market totaling over 7 million people. Supplementing these agricultural industries one also finds the usual ones given over to providing run-of-the-mill goods not requiring complex techniques: textiles, furniture, paper, glass, and some chemical products.

Minerals. Cuba possesses a greater wealth in minerals than the past record of the country would indicate. The inability to take full advantages of the available deposits camouflages their extent. Not much effort has ever been given to the exploration of minerals in Cuba. The Spanish, not finding gold in any substantial quantity, never exhibited much zeal in exploiting other minerals. After independence, the United States developed, or failed to develop, mineral industries largely in accordance with its own needs. In some cases Cuban resources were "kept on tap" as a reserve.

Nickel, iron, chromite, copper, and manganese deposits in Cuba have international significance, yet production for the first half of the 20th century averaged less than $10 million per year, about 3 percent of the value of a good year's mineral production from Arizona's mines.

The present government has not to date pushed ahead with mineral production, at least no more than before the Revolution. This policy fits in with the policy of not diversifying the Cuban economy on an appreciable scale. It is reported, however, that efforts to locate oil deposits go on.

Economy Shift. The Cuban Revolution of 1959 brought in its wake much more than a change in political theory. Established ties with the Western world, especially the United States, were summarily broken off in favor of new ties with the Soviet Bloc. Such a shift has meant what amounts to almost complete reversal in Cuba's external relations.

The natural advantages of Cuba's key location in the American Mediterranean have been sacrificed in favor of commercial relations with trading partners deep in Eurasia. Distant marketing centers in the Soviet Union and Eastern Europe have replaced the convenient trade lines from Havana and other Cuban ports to the Atlantic seaboard of the United States. Cuban air terminals are now virtual voids within the busy airline networks of the Western Hemisphere. The Cuban, Czechoslovakian, Soviet, and Spanish national airlines each have weekly flights in each direction between Havana and Europe, and there is a service to Mexico City—a far cry from the former heavy daily traffic between Havana and the airports of New York, Miami, and Key West.

Commercial relations with other Western Hemisphere areas likewise dwindled or disappeared. Petroleum, for example, now comes from the Black Sea fields rather than nearby Venezuela.

Before 1959 sinews of the entire Cuban economy were largely branded with American trademarks. They reflected the American way of doing business. Wide usage of American machinery required servicing with American parts. Stores had been stocked with American goods. Those organizations requiring heavy investments depended largely on American capital. Planeloads and boatloads of American tourists swarmed the hostelries and spas of the Havana area. To change this United States-oriented system has raised problems in Cuba and at the same time brought about an era of austerity. A gradual but relentless program of nationalizing industries, usually at the expense of the foreign and domestic entrepreneurs and management alike, brought a temporary flow of wealth to the Cuban treasury.

It is yet early to ascertain whether or not a Communist economic policy will succeed in utilizing the potential of Cuba's opulent environment. Few would question the corruptness of previous regimes, yet to date the present leadership has failed miserably to provide the Cuban population with a standard of living commensurate with the natural wealth at hand. Too, lack of individual incentive and disregard of the natural advantages of geographic location unquestionably operate against material success in the planned national economy. One new and rather drastic development to stimulate the island's economy is the decision in favor of compulsory military service for Cuban men between 17 and 45 as a source of cheap labor. Rather than military training the manpower will be assigned to agricultural work, road building, and other menial tasks.

Human Element. From earliest Spanish times the inhabitants of Cuba have been subjected to a theme of political turmoil overriding a seemingly never-ending succession of grave economic problems and crises. Prior to independence, restrictions and oppression on the part of metropole Spain led them to revolt. Since independence, resistance to external influences and pressures has strengthened their national consciousness. Subjection to the avarice and manipulation of a privileged minority endowed them with a persistent discontent toward a *status quo*. Few have been the years of prosperity or periods of sustained material progress for the people as a whole.

The basic population of Cuba can be attributed to Spanish immigration. Because of varying degrees of ethnic mixtures and subjective methods of taking census or making estimates, the racial distribution is confusing. For example, the 1953 census accounts for 72.8 percent of the total population as white (mostly of Spanish extraction), 12.4 percent as black, and 14.5 percent as mixed. Other estimates give as high as 49 percent negroid and only 30 percent as white.

Before the 1959 Revolution no serious racial problems existed, although the color line was unofficially observed socially and in employment opportunities. The new regime has made a great issue of racial equality. Such a policy may be no more than political propaganda, as exemplified by the Castro government's failing to appoint Negroes to high government posts and claiming to champion "Indian America" when Cuba has only the faintest traces of Indian blood in the population.

Approaching a population of 7.25 million (1963) Cuba has a

density greater than Indiana but less than Illinois, on the order of 150 per square mile. This figure represents more than a four-fold increase since independence some 60 years ago. Throughout rural Cuba the density is fairly consistent from geographic region to geographic region, but a strong trend toward urbanization distorts the over-all distribution. In the 1953 census 57 percent of the population were rated as urban, and there is reason to believe that this figure is steadily climbing. Havana, advancing rapidly toward the million class (897,000 in 1962), gives a density of more than 500 per square mile to its province.

The Tally. With a physical environment extremely favorable to agriculture and extractive industries Cuba has a potential difficult to evaluate by any known yardstick. In the past, attempts to develop the island in relation to this rich geographical base have failed to receive support, for governments were more interested in political prowess, personalities, and a fast turn-over of profit than in any balanced long-term planning. The recent Revolution started yet another program in which a political system supersedes all other considerations, this one all the more serious in that its repercussions extend far beyond the Cuban coastline.

Without question the Dominican Republic is the most Spanish of any political entity in the West Indies. While Columbus was yet sailing the Atlantic the island now known as Hispaniola* was selected to be the site of a colony under the flag of Spain. It towered in prestige, for through here Spain sought to build her New World empire. A shortage of gold after half a century disillusioned the Spanish government, resulting in neglect as the channels of colonization bypassed the island. Nevertheless, for the next three centuries the major influence in the eastern part of Hispaniola continued to be Spanish, establishing many of the traditions found to this day.

Factors beyond early historical events also contribute to the strong Spanish atmosphere overriding the Dominican scene. Other than the heavy proportion of Negro blood, resulting from the importation of slaves, the majority of the inhabitants trace their lineage to Spain. The Spanish language prevails throughout the island other than for tongues used by several minorities, representing groups of immigrants. Again, more than 98 percent of the people are Catholic, the religion brought directly from Spain with the first colonists. Finally, one might point to the architecture as being basically Spanish, despite certain modifications to conform with a tropical environment.

The Land. Occupying approximately the eastern two thirds of the island of Hispaniola, the area of the Dominican Republic is large for the West Indies but small in relation to measurements on

---

* Columbus named the island *La Española,* thought to have been the original version of the word "Hispaniola."

the nearby continents. Uruguay, smallest of South American countries, contains nearly four times as much territory. In the United States the states of Vermont and New Hampshire together equal the Dominican Republic in area.

Land forms of the Dominican Republic cannot be described as fitting into any symmetrical pattern. One large and three smaller ranges aligned roughly in a northwest-southeast direction cover much of the country. Flanking interior lowlands and coastal plains favor agricultural pursuits. Here also one finds all of the important cities and most lines of communication. In the north between two ranges the Cibao lowland parallels the north shore and together with tributary coastal areas provides a home for more than half the population. In the southeast a relatively wide coastal lowland, hinterland to the capital city of Santo Domingo, accounts for another one-third of the population. Most prominent physiographic feature, the rugged Cordillera Central curves southeastward from the midsection of the Dominican-Haiti boundary to the midsection of the southern shore. It has effectively separated the two populous areas and caused political cleavage within the Dominican government. Rebellions have frequently been spawned in the north, based on sectional viewpoints which reflect diverse environments.

Climatic handicaps are not pronounced over the Dominican landscape other than an occasional devastating hurricane. In the southeast some irrigation must supplement the rainfall to insure optimum sugar cane growth, but offsetting this disadvantage the greater amount of sunshine characteristic of a drier climate raises the sugar content. The driest lowland area, in the southwest in the lee of the Cordillera Central, may have an annual rainfall as low as 20 inches.

Extensive areas of high mountains means that the Dominican Republic has the coldest weather in the West Indies. Snow falls at times on some of the higher peaks, while frost is not uncommon at any elevation above 3,500 feet.

The People. In 1963 the United Nations estimated the population of the Dominican Republic to be 3,334,000, a startling increase of 370 percent in the 43 years since 1920. Such growth ranks as exceedingly high by any standard. Natural increase—high birth and low death rate—rather than immigration accounts for all but a negligible proportion of this rapid upswing. In direct contrast, the population during colonial times was low and grew slowly. At the time of independence in 1844 the total number of inhabitants probably stood at slightly more than 100,000.

Despite the unprecedented population increase in recent decades the density of 178 persons per square mile is well under half that of neighboring Haiti. A declining birth rate appears to be about the only safeguard against serious population pressure in the future, but at the present time opportunities still exist for land development.

Only three persons out of ten live in cities, but the proportion of urbanization surges upward as industry receives more emphasis. The lure of the big city is present in the Dominican Republic as in many other parts of Latin America. Santo Domingo at the beginning of the 1930's was an unimpressive town of 32,000 with mud streets. Now, with a population of around 400,000 and an array of fine buildings, it ranks as one of the most imposing metropolises of the Caribbean.

Economic Base. Most people in the Dominican Republic gain their living by agriculture in one form or another. Sugar, although the mainstay of the economy, is not an all-dominating crop. Cacao and coffee also figure strongly among the exports, their revenue together approaching that of sugar. The majority of the rural inhabitants, however, depend for their livelihood upon a system of subsistence farming. Fortunately the environment favors a wide range of fruits, vegetables, and cereals, making the average Dominican worker appear relatively well off. Large areas devoted to raising livestock further testify to a standard of living not equaled in many parts of the West Indies.

Dominican industry reflects an agricultural base, for the most important plants are for processing or manufacturing such products as sugar, molasses, rum, alcohol, chocolate, vegetable oils, cigarettes, and livestock products. Other manufactures conform to the usual pattern found in Latin American countries: textiles, shoes, brewery products, simple household items, and the ubiquitous flow of cement.

Mineral resources, while numerous in variety, are short in quantity. Lack of fuels in particular handicaps industrial development, as illustrated by the necessity to depend in part upon charcoal to generate heat both in the home and in factories. Coal exists only in the form of meager lignite deposits, while a search for petroleum, the great hope, revealed underground pools scarcely worth exploiting. In contrast, some development of hydroelectric power in the future can be expected in light of the rugged terrain and heavy rainfall over many of the slopes.

Realizing the necessity of efficient transportation, the government constructed good roads the length and breadth of the country. An effective highway net focuses upon three major roads extending west, north, and east from Santo Domingo. As a result no section of the country is isolated; anyone can get to the capital within 24 hours. Railroads never competed seriously with the country's roadways. Formerly a single rail route extended from the north coast through the Cibao plain; it is now reduced to rusting tracks between La Vega (near Santiago) and Sánchez, and these without service. A local airline serving several of the larger cities has discontinued its schedules.

Disfranchisement of Dictatorship. The year 1930 marked a sharp turn in the fortunes of the Dominican Republic. Before then progress had been a slow uphill pull. In that year, however, General Rafael Leónidas Trujillo assumed the presidency and subjected the country to a strong dictatorship, lasting until his assassination in 1961. This period of 31 years has lent itself to much discussion as to whether the Trujillo regime had any merit to offset its brutal nature. Supporters of Trujillo have advanced the claim that great material advances took place which were of benefit to the general populace as well as to the ruling cliques. However, the great majority of the population living outside of the money economy were unaffected. On the surface, at least, the country was a model of order, but based upon one man's whims rather than national laws in the accepted sense. The over-all result was a regime of deadly oppression completely void of civil liberties. A review of the pre-

Trujillo situation in the country sheds some light on how such a regime could come about.

The Dominican Republic on the eve of the Trujillo *coup d'état* had little about which it could boast. Economic chaos and political turmoil had grown to be, as it were, the order of the day although there was a period of relative stability from 1924 to 1928. After an initial period of prestige in the early 16th century as the heart of Spain's New World empire, the colony, neglected by the mother country, started on its unfortunate downward path. Until independence in 1844 it had largely to shift for itself and was subjected to armed incursions from the western end of Hispaniola. In fact, for the 22-year period prior to independence the Haitians took over the entire island, and from this situation the country received its independence.

Being their own masters brought but little relief to the hapless Dominicans, torn by civil strife most of the time. The development of agriculture and industry received but little encouragement other than for brief breathing periods between corrupt regimes and economic prostration. During the second decade of the present century the weakened condition of the country, especially its inability to honor contracted debts, brought about intervention from the United States. Some interests called for outright annexation of the republic, a movement forestalled by the U.S. Congress and public sentiment. Nevertheless, in 1916 U.S. marines landed in Santo Domingo and other cities and took over control. They remained for eight years while efforts were made to strengthen the Dominican government. Order was maintained and some economic progress was effected, but in retrospect the episode appears in a bad light. Dominicans resented the presence of the heavy hand of the "Colossus of the North," as did other citizens in the Latin American community. After the marines departed, further disorders were somewhat tempered by a period of relative prosperity common to the entire Western Hemisphere. But by 1930 the situation, accentuated by low sugar prices, had further deteriorated, this time supplemented by a disastrous hurricane sweeping over the eastern end of the island and virtually destroying the capital city. Here was the sorrowful picture of a small republic which had just about reached the end of the road.

The ensuing dictatorship appeared to lift the material welfare of the Dominican Republic, but no real advance took place until the boom years of the war and postwar periods. For example, 17 years were required to eliminate the foreign debt. The new regime purported to adopt a number of progressive measures, such as one designed to promote industrial development by offering tax concessions. However, the effort expended amounted largely to window dressing, for the only industrial development was for the benefit of Trujillo and carried out on the basis of hidden subsidies. The majority of the installations of that time have since proved unprofitable to operate without the subsidies. Exports did increase, partly due to better transportation facilities. Accompanying this newly found paper prosperity the country took on a glossy look with such devices as fine new buildings, parks, and statues. Later in the Trujillo regime a strong bid was made for tourism by the erection of attractive luxury hotels and a welcome mat for visitors. This campaign, without question, proved to be a failure; the tourists just did not come.

The instigator of the aforementioned fanfare took full credit for accomplishments under the label of "His Excellency the Generalisimo and Dr. Rafael Leónidas Trujillo, Benefactor of the Fatherland." Under the guise of this salutory title, however, he operated by an iron rule in which no opposition was tolerated. Even the mild-sounding words of objective text describing the political measures taken could not cover the deep-seated ruthlessness of the Trujillo Regime: "Since 1948 the President has been given extraordinary powers to regulate by decree and without congressional approval all matters concerning national security and welfare, culminating in 1951 when he was given powers to declare a national emergency and to suspend the constitutional checks on the executive." * As might be evaluated by any type of yardstick used in a

* *The Statesman's Yearbook, 1961-62,* St. Martin's Press, New York.

democracy, the social cost was dear indeed for any slight progress which might have taken place during these years.

Since the death of the "Benefactor" the Dominican Republic has been going through a difficult period of adjustment. On the economic side the country can count many blessings in having been raised above the level of a grinding poverty. But political tension continues to run high, and at one period, September-December 1963, relations with the United States became significantly strained.* Transition to a democratic form of government is proving difficult despite the rank hatred expressed in the country toward the former dictator.

As is true in Cuba, the geographic development of the Dominican Republic has been subordinated to a marked degree by political factors. Exploitation of resources and the pattern of sequent occupance was in turn controlled by an unsympathetic metropole government, stifled by internecine politics, and encouraged by a regime void of civil liberties. The result is an economy primarily agrarian despite a veneer of commerce and industry. Future governments should find a potential well worth pursuing.

* One of the bench marks of Trujillo's ability to survive was his friendly attitude toward the United States. This ironic situation made open criticism of the Trujillo regime by Americans somewhat awkward, although during three periods the dictator slackened off with his friendliness: 1930-1931, 1939-1941, and 1960-1961.

9   *Haiti*

HAITI declared independence in 1804, making it the first independent state in Latin America. In fact, statehood in Haiti followed that in the United States by only 28 years. Not until another 40 years had passed did another sovereign state, the Dominican Republic, emerge in the West Indies. Still more than another half century elapsed before Cuba, the third West Indian nation, came into being. Early independence, however, proved far from a solution to colonial troubles, as any probing into this Caribbean country's history will verify.

Occupying only the western part of an island, Haiti has by the nature of this position suffered by a conflict of interests with the eastern part. During colonial times French interests in the west clashed with Spain's stake in the east. After independence the troubles have developed primarily from internal tension. Actual or potential danger of thrusts from one side of the island to the other have commonly been from west to east. A dynamic history in the western end undoubtedly gave impetus to thrusts in this direction, but more basic has been the pressure of population. As late as 1937 a major border holocaust took some 10,000 lives when workers from Haiti were massacred in the Dominican Republic. Tension remains high, the boundary clamped shut from time to time, and threats fly back and forth between Port-au-Prince and Santo Domingo. On the other hand, some effort toward lessening the friction between the two countries has recently been making headway under the threat of a possible invasion of Hispaniola from Cuba.

One-Third of an Island.   In area Haiti is little more than one half as large as the Dominican Republic. Its highly irregular outline further restricts distances within the country. Every point is within 35 miles of either the sea or the Dominican boundary. In fact, Port-au-Prince, a "west coast" city, lies only 22 miles from Haiti's eastern boundary.

The mountain ranges readily identified in the Dominican Republic extend irregularly across the boundary to give Haiti its basic physical structure. Two of them continue eastward as peninsulas, the northern one for 50 miles in the direction of Cuba and the southern for nearly 200 miles in the direction of Jamaica. Maximum elevations, however, fail by about 2,000 feet to reach those of the Dominican Republic. Although the relief in Haiti generally appears jumbled on the map, three lowland areas of major significance can be seen wedged within the rugged mountainous framework. One, in the extreme northeast, and first attracting settlers to the eastern part of Hispaniola, is an extension of the Cibao section of the Dominican Republic. Another, known by the expressive French term, *Cul de sac,* serves as a hinterland for Port-au-Prince. The third lies in the valley of the Artibonite River about midway between the other two lowlands.

The rough and broken nature of Haiti's surface strongly marks the cultural development and potential of the environment. Deep indentations along the coastline form bays and harbors and have provided the country with at least a dozen ports. Less favorable, the many steep slopes have created a complex climatic pattern, including several disagreeable features. Those areas in the lee of mountain ranges fail to receive sufficient rainfall for raising crops. Some pockets, blocked from the refreshing relief of the trade winds, suffer hot and muggy weather conditions reminiscent of the Amazon Valley. The windward and consequently wetter sides of the mountains still have extensive areas of forest lands. At higher elevations these may be extensive stands of pine.

Composition of the Population.   Haitians differ markedly from any other nationality in all of Latin America. Negroes make up, according to estimates, from 90 to 95 percent of the total population. Almost all of the remainder are considered as "colored," that is, mulatto, from a mixture of Negro and white blood. The cleavage between black and dark brown people on the one hand and light—in many cases almost white—people on the other has given rise to many internal problems. The latter group, for the most part comprising the elite, is continuously being challenged by those with darker skins, some of whom also qualify as elite in status. There is obviously no sharp line of distinction between the two groups, but the resentment against those with darker skins trying to forge ahead socially and politically have been given credit for causing many of the civil wars and revolutions in the country.

Pressure of Population. Haiti's population density of 415 persons per square mile becomes more meaningful in light of the extensive mountainous area of the country. A fair estimate of the density in the lower elevations, where the great majority of the people live, would approach 1,500 persons per square mile. A total of 4,448,000 people (mid-1963 United Nations estimate) presses sorely upon the resources which with but few exceptions are limited to stretches of fertile soil and a tropical climate capable of supporting vegetative growth. No other country in Latin America has so low a per capita income—well under $100 per year. Inhabitants of Great Bend, Kansas, drive about the same number of passenger automobiles as are found in all of Haiti.

Rural population exceeds that of urban areas by a ratio of more than seven to one. Other than the capital city of Port-au-Prince, now approaching one-quarter million, Haiti has no city with a population of more than 30,000. Small towns and villages, however, abound, scattered throughout the country as marketing centers and distribution outlets for the simple trade needs of the vast numbers of people.

Social Structure. By U.S. standards fully nine-tenths of the people in Haiti live in poverty, depending largely on what they can produce by tending their fragmented farms. The best that can be said is that farmers generally own the land on which they work and at least escape the tribulations of tenantry. Around a type of self-sufficient rural economy a fantastic marketing system has evolved, operated largely by the women of local communities. Dealing in commodities of infinitesimal value, they buy and sell tremendous numbers and varieties of items. Established marketing centers abound, while on fixed days of the week teeming bazaar-like market places may spring up along otherwise little-developed roadways. Produce from nearby farms is obviously hawked, but in addition household goods and farm supplies enter into the bartering: candles, kerosene, piece goods, salt, combs, and so on. Among the products raised for sale are commercial crops, which in total count among the country's leading exports.

At the other end of the social scale the elite, amounting to no more than two or three percent of the population, live in relative luxury. They comprise the top echelons in the bureaucratic, professional, and commercial worlds. Frequently educated abroad and well traveled, they have brought to the Haitian scene some of the elegance of continental sophistication. They take special pride in speaking cultured French rather than Creole.

A weakness in Haiti's social structure lies in the lack of any substantial intermediate class between the elite and the underprivileged masses. The relatively insignificant middle class that does exist comprises a few tens of thousands of low-echelon government employees; the better paid workers in commerce, industry, and agriculture; and domestic servants.

Christianity in the form of the Catholic religion encompasses the Haitian elite, resulting from the missionary stress of early colonization. Among the masses of the population, however, it never took root sufficiently to suppress the type of pagan worship practiced by many of the people, especially peasants. Known as Voodoo, or Vodun, these ancient rites hark back to the African homeland from which originated past generations of so many of the present inhabitants. Despite their primitive manifestations the dances and rituals performed are more of a cult than mere expressions of superstition; they never have been far below the surface. In recent years Voodoo ceremonies, seance-like in their execution, have come more to the attention of the outside world, even to the extent of becoming tourist attractions.

Unimpressive Economy. In contrast to most West Indian lands sugar cane does not rank as the leading source of income. Although the proportions vary from year to year, coffee leads as the main trading item. Either sugar or sisal ranks as a poor second. However, the value of Haiti's coffee exports per capita, representing about one-half of the total for the country, is only about one-fourth of the Dominican Republic's sugar exports per capita. In each case these crops represent about two-fifths of the total export trade of their respective countries.

Industrial development progresses but slowly as a bolster to the Haitian economy. Manufacturing, although encouraged by governmental action, has not advanced far beyond the processing of domestic crops, fabrication of some of the country's essential needs, and making of handicraft articles for sale to tourists.

Some potential for industry rests in exploiting mineral resources, of which the country has appreciable deposits of a variety, including bauxite, manganese, copper, and low-grade coal. Local capital and technical skill have apparently not been equal to the task of establishing mineral industries, and outside interests have so far been slow in coming.

Lack of a modern transportation system handicaps any attempt to strengthen the economy. Rugged terrain and heavy vegetation have delayed interregional communications. Roads offer the only practical means of surface travel about the country. Although roads extend to all parts of Haiti, including the extremities of the two peninsulas, traveling conditions remain primitive, especially during rainy weather.

Water and air travel serve to supplement transportation over the land. Domestic shipping is facilitated by 850 miles of coastline, one mile for every 12.5 square miles of territory. Haiti's two prominent peninsulas are responsible for such a high ratio of shore to area. Small vessels carry cargo along the coast, but seem to have a propensity for sinking! A local airline connects Port-au-Prince with seven other cities, forming a radial air route pattern. The aircraft are operated by the military with from two to six schedules per week over each route.

Political and Economic Heritage. Among the states of Latin America the Republic of Haiti has the weakest economy if one measures it by the some $70 gross national product per capita. Further, the government continues to show signs of political instability. During the early 1960's an increasingly rigid authoritarian regime brought the country to the brink of open revolt. In the face of an extreme pressure of population upon the modest resources of the country it becomes difficult to distinguish cause and effect in analyzing national ills.

The present predicament in which Haiti finds itself is undoubtedly borrowed from the past. During the more than four and a half centuries since Columbus set foot on the northern shores of Hispaniola the fortunes of the east end of this island have tended to run bad rather than good. Only in the early years of French colonialism, after the Treaty of Ryswick in 1697, does history relate bright and prosperous times. Saint-Domingue (Haiti's name at that time) was purported to be one of the richest colonies in the world. Great sugar estates, supported by several hundred thousand slaves (465,429 in 1789), produced much revenue for France.

Yet in the background the picture of a few thousand white settlers living in grand style constituted an imbalance of economic standards among the inhabitants which wracked Haiti with so much turmoil and devastation. Well before the end of the first century of colonization the Spanish had decimated the original population of nearly a million Arawaks. The stage was thus set for the importation of slaves to do the work of the French who took over the area the following century. It was unfortunate for the welfare of the colony that the French Revolution took place at a time when Negro slaves outnumbered the white population by more than 15 to 1. Strong men among the slaves were able to lead a successful revolution and gain independence, but 12 years of fighting resulted in the destruction of the economic structure developed by the French colonials. Since this time recurrent internal power struggles have not permitted any sustained period of economic growth, nor has foreign capital been attracted as in other parts of the Caribbean.

Early in the present century internal conditions deteriorated to the point that the United States sent in Marine occupation forces. During their stay, from 1915-1934, there is no question but what order was restored and many material improvements were effected. Nevertheless, it is not at all certain that this action could be construed as successful. Much resentment was evidenced against the occupation, not alone by the Haitians, and over the long haul no improvement in the country's economic policies appeared to evolve.

10   *Jamaica*

J AMAICA took its place among the independent nations of the world on August 6, 1962, after more than three centuries of British rule. Membership in the Commonwealth after independence, however, has assured continued ties with the United
Kingdom, as indicated by the island's excellent trade and diplo-
matic relations with the former metropole.

Columbus claimed the island for Spain in 1494 on his second
voyage to the New World. Spanish colonization proved weak, and
little development took place beyond establishment of a few cattle
ranches to furnish supplies for expeditions to mainland America.
In 1655 the English captured Jamaica, but some years passed before
all the Spaniards were driven out. In fact, Spain did not formally
cede Jamaica to the English Crown until 1670.

As was typical in the West Indies, the island became a sugar
producer, flourishing until the abolition of the slave trade in 1807
and of slave labor in 1834. Planters found it impossible to compete
with Cuba and other islands which retained slavery for the time.
Many of the freed slaves headed for the hills, and plantation labor
became so short that workers were brought in from China and
India. A series of bitter disputes between landowners and laborers,
which culminated in the short-lived but bloody Morant Bay Rebellion in 1865, called for a drastic overhaul of the island's administration. The subsequent reorganization of the government resulted
in far more control being exercised by the British Crown. The resulting years of authority from London furnished a much-needed
political rest period during which both the political and the economic milieu began to improve.

Administration of Jamaican affairs was passed, little by little, to
the people of the island, and by the 1930's political organizations

were beginning to advocate complete self-government for Jamaica. In 1947, this trend got sidetracked for a time when representatives of all the British Caribbean peoples met at Montego to consider uniting the British West Indies under a single federal government. After numerous conferences, much study, and countless debates, most of the British colonies in the West Indies agreed, in 1956, to federate and to work toward the creation of a single, fully independent nation. Thus, in 1958, the federation, confusingly called The West Indies, was formally established. After only three years the Jamaicans decided in a referendum to pull out from the embryonic federation and to "go it alone."

Land and Climate. Although it is by far the largest English-speaking Caribbean island, Jamaica with 4,411 square miles is considerably smaller than Connecticut. Mountains cover much of the surface; about half of the terrain exceeds 1,000 feet elevation, and individual peaks reach above 7,000 feet. Numerous rivers in the higher eastern side of the island carry great quantities of water during the rainy season, and they have carved out deep valleys. Because of steep gradients few of the rivers are navigable for more than very short stretches, and because their flow is not constant throughout the year most of them have not been exploited for hydroelectric power.

Jamaica's coastal plains are most extensive along the southern and western parts of the island, where they extend as much as 15 miles inland. Along the north coast they are generally restricted to a narrow zone crowded between limestone cliffs and the sea. These coastal lowlands, with few exceptions, contain highly productive soil and support a dense population.

The parallel of 18 degrees North Latitude passes through the city of Kingston. This position in the midst of the warm Caribbean means that the temperature is either warm or hot, depending on the metabolism of the reporter. The thermometer varies but little from season to season; the "extremes" that do exist are from place to place about the island. For instance, on the southeast coast temperatures vary from about 70° F. (a "cool day") to 90° F. (a "hot day"), averaging about 80° F. Most of the 90 degree weather, naturally enough, comes during the summer, but it is not uncommon to have such high temperatures in the midst of the winter; nor is it uncommon to have relatively cool weather in the summertime. By contrast, temperatures at Blue Mountain Peak, 7,400 feet above sea level, range from a mean maximum of 69° F. to a mean minimum of 43° F. with not much variation from month to month. In the center of the island at an altitude of about 3,000 feet it becomes sufficiently cool, especially at night, to require the visitor to switch from shorts and a light shirt to long trousers and a sweater.

Rainfall contrasts from place to place surpass those of temperature. The mountain slopes bearing the brunt of the northerly and easterly winds receive heavy precipitation; the plains shielded by the mountains receive the least. Thus, Port Antonio on the northeast coast receives about 127 inches annually; Kingston, on the south coast in the rainshadow of the Blue Mountains, averages less than 30 inches. This relatively light rainfall along the wide coastal strip forces the farmers to rely at least in part upon irrigation.

Population and Population Movements. Most of the 1,684,000 people in Jamaica live on the coastal lowlands and in the interior basins. The higher mountains are but sparsely settled, and a few unusual places such as the Cockpit Country* are almost empty. About one-fifth of the total population lives in the Kingston metropolitan area. The second and third cities, Montego Bay and Spanish Town, though of special tourist interest, have but 25,000 and 17,000 inhabitants respectively.

The population of Jamaica has almost doubled over the past 40 years; in 1920 there were only some 855,000 people living on the island. This remarkable increase has come about despite the considerable outpouring of Jamaicans to other parts of the world. Jamaicans were employed in work on the Panama Canal in the early part of this century, and many of them remained in Panama. The banana plantations in lowland Costa Rica and Honduras were a source of jobs for many Jamaicans; they also streamed into Cuba during the expansion of the sugar plantations on that island. Prior to World War II a sizeable Jamaican colony had developed in New

---

* The Cockpit Country, sometimes played up in the tourist literature as a sort of forbidden "wonderland," consists of karst topography, with highly irregular elevations and depressions carved out of limestone.

York City, but this movement was essentially choked off by post-war immigration laws. At about the same time improved economic opportunities in the United Kingdom seem to have deflected the mass emigration movement eastward across the Atlantic, although contract farm laborers from Jamaica continued to go to the United States at the rate of 4,000 to 5,000 per year during the 1956-1959 period.

In 1953 some 2,200 migrants went to Great Britain; in 1955 and again in 1956 the figure exceeded 17,000. The exodus slackened somewhat during the next several years, largely because an economic recession in the United Kingdom weakened the demand for labor. In 1959 the trend again moved upward with as many as 60,000 Jamaicans thought to have migrated to the metropole in 1961. In fact, a West Indian "colony," consisting largely of Jamaicans, centered in the Knightsbridge section of London, smaller than but reminiscent of the Puerto Rican section in New York City's mid-Manhattan. In the summer of 1962 this heavy outflow from Jamaica came to an end, stopped by the Commonwealth Immigrants Act passed by the British parliament. During the preceding months great numbers migrated in a "beat-the-ban" rush.

Despite these intermittent "thinning" movements, population pressure remains extremely high in Jamaica. In fact, the population per square mile here approaches that of notoriously crowded Haiti, reaching in excess of 350 people per square mile on an island-wide basis, and almost 2,500 persons per square mile of arable land. Not only are the rural parts of the island overcrowded, but the cities and towns are densely packed. The situation is particularly critical in the Kingston-St. Andrew metropolitan area. It has been reliably estimated that within that area some 120,000 people occupy substandard dwelling units, and at least 10,000 of these are squatters living in the poorest of shacks, known in Jamaica as "tatoos." A similar lack of adequate housing and sanitary facilities exists in varying degrees elsewhere in Jamaica. For this reason, the Government of Jamaica has made the alleviation of such slum conditions the primary goal in its present development program.

Diversity of the Economy. Although Jamaicans depend upon crop-raising as the backbone of their economy, they engage in many other activities. Actually, about one-half of the people are employed in agriculture, but well over one-half of the island's earnings comes from other sources. Mining, manufacturing, construction, trade, public administration, and transportation are also important, all contributing to make the economy one of the most diversified in the Caribbean.

Sugar and its by-product, rum, account for about one-half of the island's agricultural exports. Sugar has been an important export item for many years, although not always in first place. Some three-fifths of the sugar is grown on large estates; the remainder comes from small farms which truck the harvested cane to one or another of the 20 large-estate mills for processing. In 1962, 434,000 tons of sugar were produced, of which approximately four-fifths was exported.

While sugar cane flourishes principally on the coastal plains at the eastern end of Jamaica and to the west of Kingston, bananas grow extensively throughout the island. About 80 percent of them, however, originate in the hilly country and help the regional balance of the farm economy. Principal suppliers of bananas are the operators of small farms who market their crop through cooperatives. Notwithstanding numerous plant diseases and a series of years with unfavorable weather conditions, exports have exceeded 10 million stems for the past several years to rank the crop second in earnings.

Other crops may be divided among those important for export and the mainstays produced for domestic use. The former category includes coffee, cacao, citrus fruits, and tobacco. In recent years the production of food for local consumption has been increasing at the rate of 6 percent annually, but at least 8 percent is needed to keep pace with population growth and the need for an improved nutritional level. These local crops include root crops (such as sweet potatoes and cassava), maize, pulses, rice, and coconuts. Many foods, nevertheless, must be imported, especially rice, corn, potatoes, and beans.

Bauxite Bonanza. Mining of bauxite is one of Jamaica's most important economic activities. This ore, along with alumina (a processed concentrate), has in recent years replaced sugar as the island's leading export. In fact, Jamaica ranks fifth in the world in bauxite production after the Soviet Union, Surinam, British Guiana and France. With the demand for aluminum on the upswing prospects for this extractive industry in Jamaica augur well—one of the few specialized commodities in the West Indies which has given fresh hope to Caribbean economy. Four firms, three American and one Canadian, operate the industry. The first shipment was made only in 1952; export of ore and alumina together in the early 1960's reached the order of 7.5 million tons per annum. The bauxite goes principally to the United States, where it satisfies about one-half the demand for aluminum products.

Other mineral industries, although dwarfed by bauxite, include the mining and exporting of gypsum and small-scale phosphate mining. Beyond this restricted list there has been little activity with mineral resources other than the prospecting for oil, iron ore, copper, and marble.

Prospects, Self-evaulated. Jamaicans take special pride in their lack of racial prejudices. They have created "one people out of many" and are setting about building their newly independent country into a land of opportunity for all. Perhaps one of the best ways of characterizing the current outlook for Jamaica is to list the problems the Jamaicans themselves consider of prime importance. These problems have not only been identified and examined critically; they are on the road (a long road, admittedly) to being solved. The list:

1. The alleviation of slums;
2. The provision of an adequate supply of water for domestic and farm use;
3. The expansion of education, particularly technical training;
4. The increase of agricultural production;
5. The expansion and improvement of health and sanitary facilities; and
6. The creation of more jobs and diversification of the economy through increased industrialization.

11   *Trinidad and Tobago*

THE newest state in the Western Hemisphere, Trinidad and Tobago, received its independence in August 1962.* After being groomed to play a key role in an independent West Indies federation, its sudden shift to independent status came as a surprise.† But after Jamaica had dropped out of the abortive federation, the leaders in the Trinidad government wanted no part of a federation of the eastern Caribbean along with Barbados and the Leeward and Windward islands.

Trinidad and Tobago with a combined area of only 1,980 square miles is one of the world's smallest countries. In size it exceeds only Zanzibar, Western Samoa, Luxembourg, and the microstates of Europe. Its population of 859,000, however, surpasses that of 13 other countries, including Iceland, Gabon, and Cyprus. Nonetheless, Trinidad and Tobago may be considered small even among the islands of the West Indies. Its area is only about 60 percent as large as Puerto Rico, smallest of the Greater Antilles. Aircraft landing at Piarco, aerodrome for Port of Spain, are only 20 miles from the coast on the opposite side of the island!

At its closest point the island of Trinidad lies only seven miles from the mainland of South America. In fact, its geological structure is an extension of the big continent to the south rather than that of the curving archipelago to the north and west. Three small ranges—Northern, Central, and Southern—stretch across Trinidad

---

* Trinidad and Tobago is the official name of the state, though Trinidad alone frequently serves as the short form.

† After much controversy, Port of Spain, capital of the colony of Trinidad, was to have become capital of the new federation.

to provide the physiographic framework of the island. Their maximum elevation, 3,085 feet in the Northern Mountains, is low by West Indian standards.

Tobago, 19 miles to the north, has long been associated with Trinidad because of its location. It is inconvenient of access from any other land surface. With only 116 square miles, the island is little more than an 18-mile-long mountain rising out of the sea.

As the southernmost of all West Indian islands, Trinidad is somewhat warmer than the mean for the archipelago. This location also places it out of reach of all hurricanes—a distinct advantage in the West Indies. Directly in the path of the trade winds, the island receives a maximum rainfall of 150 inches per year in the northeast. The most sheltered part of the island, in the extreme northwest, still receives nearly 50 inches. Ideal for agriculture, the precipitation nevertheless fails to provide the island with water in sufficient quantity to store for normal domestic and industrial needs.

Few parts of Trinidad are inhospitable to human habitation or at least to some useful economic activity. Forests cover about half the island, supplying a continuous source of timber. Only swamp areas on the east and west coasts preclude development of some type. On the western side of the island, between the Northern and Central mountains, one finds the greatest concentration of population, including the capital, with its nearly 100,000 persons.

Manifold Ethnology. Trinidad helps to give the West Indies the characteristics of an ethnological museum. Nearly half of the inhabitants are Negroes, harking back to early colonial days of slavery. Asiatics represent the second most important element of the population, amounting to over a third of the total. They came as indentured labor in the early part of the 18th century following the abolition of slavery by the British Parliament. The majority of this group from the Indian subcontinent were Hindus, but some were Moslems, these two religions presently being reflected in both churches and schools. The remaining inhabitants are largely of mixed blood, with small minorities of white and Chinese, the former made up principally of Spanish, French, British, and Portuguese stock.

On the streets of Trinidad's cities one hears English as a rule, but Hindi, Spanish, and a local French dialect are still in use. Despite such an admixture of contrasting races the melting pot in Trinidad has worked extremely well, and disorder occasioned by specific racial interests is rare.

Economic Bases. Without question minerals constitute Trinidad's greatest source of wealth. Petroleum accounts for more than three-quarters of the country's exports and provides one-third of the government revenue. A rapid upswing in production, partly brought about by newly developed offshore wells in the Gulf of Paria, amounts to an impressive average of 134,000 barrels daily. Among Commonwealth countries only Canada exceeds this figure.

Production is only half the story of oil in Trinidad, for the amount refined is more than twice as much as that produced. Crude petroleum imported originates not only in the nearby Maracaibo region of Venezuela, but also in the faraway Persian Gulf area. The great Texaco refinery at Pointe-à-Pierre, near Trinidad's second city of San Fernando, is the largest in the Commonwealth.

Along with petroleum deposits are important reserves of natural gas, used to good advantage in Trinidad's industries. Most interesting as well as oldest known of Trinidad's mineral resources is the pitch lake, also near San Fernando. A seemingly inexhaustible supply of natural asphalt comes from this 100-acre bog, where underground seepage replaces material removed.

It is unfortunate that these sources of mineral wealth require less labor than do agricultural pursuits of comparable worth. Despite the high revenues attributable to exploitation of petroleum, natural gas, and natural asphalt, the unemployment figures in Trinidad make depressing statistics.

If Trinidad had no mineral wealth whatsoever, its agricultural base would still insure the island an economy capable of sustaining its inhabitants. For example, annual sugar cane production of more than 200,000 tons in recent years, if rated in proportion to national area, roughly approximates that of Cuba. Cacao, the second crop, outranked sugar in production in the early part of the century before being plagued by low prices and a severe plant disease. Other

crops include citrus fruits, bananas, coffee, tobacco, coconuts, and
rice, providing the bases for some exports as well as contributing to
an agreeable standard of living.

A fortunate geographic position plus a smiling tropical environment provides an excellent base whereby Trinidad and Tobago may
prosper as one of the world's half a hundred newly emerged independent states (since World War II). The gauntlet it must run for
success includes restrictions on trade, unstable world prices, and an
internal economy not always in balance for the best interests of the
population as a whole.

12

British West Indies

E NGLAND early challenged Spain's monopoly in the West Indies. By the end of the 16th century vessels carrying representatives of His Majesty's Government as well as not-so-official adventurers and privateers were busy in the Caribbean. For more than two centuries they contested for territory up and down the Spanish Main, with particular emphasis in the Lesser Antilles. History surrounding those stormy waters is replete with accounts of islands falling first into the hands of one country and then another —the British more often than not as either the successful claimants or the vanquished.

During the 19th century, when Spain lost so much territory by the surge of independence which swept through Latin America, the British retained their possessions. They may well have been more skillful colonizers than the Spanish, but the more probable explanation is that with the exception of Jamaica the British islands were too small to support independence movements of any scope. British involvement in West Indian affairs remains with little evidence of slackening interest. The Union Jack does not presently wave over many square miles of land area in the Caribbean, but British influence is the strongest of any stemming from across the Atlantic.

Demise of a Federation. The long-heralded and much-publicized West Indian federation came into existence in 1958, after more than a decade of careful preparation and countless sessions at the conference table. The London government bolstered the emerging entity with a generous proportion of local autonomy, and until 1962 it appeared that the 10 British colonies would enter the world community flying a single flag. However, the geographic basis of such a major political venture militated against success despite the energy contributed by colony and metropole alike.

First, the 10 colonies (reading the map clockwise: Jamaica, St. Kitts Nevis and Anguilla, Antigua, Montserrat, Dominica, St. Lucia, St. Vincent, Barbados, Grenada, and Trinidad and Tobago)* were strung out in a 1,250-mile arc. Contact and assembly were difficult, for merely to call a meeting of representatives from the various colonies was in itself an expensive and awkward operation. Second, and probably the greatest deterrent to success, Jamaica and Trinidad and Tobago, the two largest and most economically viable colonies, resented the idea of having to subsidize the smaller and less well endowed colonies. Also, unrestricted movement of population would bring numbers of unwanted laborers from the small to the two large islands. A third, less evident, factor lay in the low living standards of all the colonies and the pressure of population which would work against any accumulation of capital to use in promoting economic progress. Would not any hard-fought material improvement in the welfare of the new state be immediately absorbed by the rampant increase in population? Could the little band of colonies "make a go of it" under a single administration with such a potential handicap? One unsympathetic British statesman facetiously declared that the federation was no more than "a pooling of poverty."

At any rate, the federation never saw the light of day as an independent state. First Jamaica and then Trinidad and Tobago made decisions to launch forth as separate sovereign nations. Accordingly, The West Indies federation was dissolved on May 31, 1962; Jamaica and Trinidad and Tobago joined the world community of nations a few months later (August 6 and 31 respectively) amid joyous fanfare.

The "Little Seven."   With the break-up of the ill-fated federation seven of the remaining eight colonies, known as the "Little Seven" (Antigua, Barbados, Dominica, Montserrat, St. Kitts Nevis and

---

* The British Virgin Islands and the Bahamas never figured beyond conjecture in the federation's blueprint, nor did the British dependencies on the mainland, British Honduras and British Guiana.

Anguilla, St. Lucia, and St. Vincent) considered formation of an Eastern Caribbean Federation, while Barbados has gone on record as favoring independence, either with or without the other six colonies. Apart, Grenada favored joining Trinidad and Tobago as a division of that unitary state. Notwithstanding the string of issues and search for solution, little if any real headway in this direction has as yet materialized. If one takes stock of the meagerly endowed geographic environment upon which a successful federation could be built, the problems facing the ambitious little political entities become ominous. Without some political action, however, they may well slide back to pre-1958 days, with no advantages accruing from community organization.

The eight colonies remaining from the dissolved The West Indies federation, including their dependencies, extend from 18° to 12° North Latitude, a distance of more than 450 miles. (See Appendix, Table 3, for tabulation of sovereignties and islands.) But in area their combined surface of 1,317 square miles would not cover much more than the state of Rhode Island. Individually, the colonies range in size from Dominica with 290 square miles to tiny Montserrat with only 32 square miles. Some stand alone, such as Barbados and St. Lucia; others have smaller islands attached to them administratively, such as the Grenadines which are divided between Grenada and St. Vincent. St. Kitts Nevis and Anguilla is a single colony formed by three islands and one dependency (Sombrero), even though Nevis and Anguilla lie 115 miles apart.* Some of the islands are low, or at least have substantial proportions of their area either flat or rolling, while others are essentially mountain peaks emerging from the sea. The generally irregular terrain does at least provide the islands with natural harbor sites that have long made them readily accessible.

Although the islands vary in physical detail, their similarity of location, a common climate, and the same general historical sequence give the colonies and life on them many like characteristics.

---

* St. Kitts is also known as St. Christopher. Note that St. Kitts Nevis and Anguilla, the official name of the colony, is properly written without punctuation.

Limited areas of fertile soil along with a moderately wet tropical climate made the islands attractive sites for sugar plantations. In turn, descendants of slaves imported from Africa to provide labor form the major part of today's population.

The imprint of the population is monotonously the same from island to island, that of pressure upon available resources to the point where nearly everyone is poor. The per capita income in Barbados is only $250, or one-half that of nearby Trinidad. Widespread differences do exist, however, in the number of people any given colony will support. Dominica, with 62,000 inhabitants, carries a density of 213 per square mile, extremely low for the Lesser Antilles. Barbados, on the other hand, with 235,000 inhabitants, challenges demographers with 1,415 persons per square mile. On Dominica as well as on Barbados the land is crowded, for only a fraction of the former island's surface is capable of agricultural development.

A "Little Seven" federation may come into being. Or the islands could be put under the auspices of the United Nations, possibly as a type of trust territory.* Or they might remain as colonies for an indeterminate period, with a maximum of local autonomy as the British have been prone to grant their dependent areas. But whatever the solution—or lack of a solution—the islands themselves must take the initiative in finding a means of survival, and beyond that, of striving for economic progress. Partial answers include greater efficiency in producing agricultural commodities for export, diversification of crops for domestic use, development of community manufacturing to cut down imports, improvement of the fishing industry, further augmentation of tourism, and, probably most important of all, the widespread practice of birth control. Grants in aid, area projects sponsored by commissions, and other types of international cooperation are obviously helpful, but the building up of confidence by which to attract outside capital probably offers the greatest potential means of stimulating constructive development.

---

* The recent swing toward independence for all dependent areas may strongly encourage some action to eliminate colonies in any part of the Free World.

THE BAHAMAS

Bahamans claim that their islands lie outside the West Indies. Certainly Atlantic rather than Caribbean waters wash the shores of the low-lying archipelago, and the low coralline limestone formation contrasts strongly with the towering structure of the Greater Antilles to the south. Nevertheless, the Bahamas, roughly paralleling the Cuban coast for about 750 miles, are popularly linked with the Caribbean by association.

Even though careful historical research places Columbus' initial landfall in the New World on the Bahaman island of San Salvador (Watlings Island), nearly a century and a half was to pass before any Europeans became sufficiently interested in the island group to permanently entrench themselves there. The first settlements were on the more favorable islands, especially Eleuthera. Negroes, largely comprising runaway slaves, settled to the south, in the poor swampy areas. This cleavage of color tends to remain to the present day, although the black and mulatto population makes up about four-fifths of the total.

Paucity of resources and a relatively low rainfall prevented the Bahamas from enjoying the wealth of sugar production as did islands to the south and east. Two brief periods of prosperity were enjoyed, however. First, during the American Revolution, cotton brought premium prices, and later, during the Civil War, a lucrative business in blockade running and bootlegging developed. In more recent years the only windfall has been the spectacular upswing of tourist trade. Nassau, the capital and center of attraction, drew 368,000 visitors in 1962 compared to only 32,000 in 1949. So many Americans visit this "offshore Miami Beach" that machines vending Bahaman stamps require U.S. coins! About the only other important source of revenue is the export of lumber and pulpwood from the extensive pine forests on the islands.

The aforementioned cleavage between white and black has been the paramount problem in local government. The white party has largely been responsible for developing the booming tourist traffic and has been in power. But there has been enough unrest among the black party to suggest a serious internal shake-up. In 1964 the British granted the islands complete self government, which should insure a greater degree of domestic stability.

BRITISH VIRGIN ISLANDS

The British Virgin Islands cannot be distinguished geographically from the Virgin Islands of the United States, for together they form a single continuous archipelago. In fact, a strait less than three-fourths of a mile in width separates islands of the two groups. With few exceptions the surface of the some 32 islands making up the British colony are steep and mountainous. The combined area of 59 square miles is small even among the Lesser Antilles. Fewer than 7,500 people live on the 11 islands that are inhabited.

Adverse physical conditions make life difficult for the Virgin Islanders. A livelihood is eked out by such simple activities as a shifting cultivation of vegetables, raising livestock in the scrubby woodland pasture, and producing charcoal. Charlotte Amalie, the chief commercial center of the American Virgin Islands, also serves as the principal British Virgin Island entrepôt.

TURKS AND CAICOS ISLANDS

Probably the most obscure political entities in the entire West Indian area are the small, flat Turks and Caicos Islands. Here live in unspectacular fashion about 6,000 people on eight more or less featureless islands. Geographically the two groups form a southeastern extension of the Bahama Islands.

Prior to the formation of the West Indies federation they were administratively attached to the Colony of Jamaica. During the federation (1958-1962) they constituted a territory within The West Indies and the governor of Jamaica was also governor of the Turks and Caicos. With the dissolution of the federation and an independent Jamaica they now comprise a British Colony in fact, although documentation to this effect is difficult to find. Presumably their destiny in any future moves toward independence will parallel those of the other colonies in the British West Indies.

13

French West Indies

Situated in the heart of the Lesser Antilles lie Martinique and Guadeloupe, forming what may conveniently be called the French West Indies. Martinique stands alone, but to Guadeloupe must be added its dependencies of Marie Galante, La Désirade, Les Saints, St. Barthélemy, and part of St. Martin.* In physical arrangement these islands do not stand as a group. Dominica, a British Colony despite its Latin-sounding name, lies midway between Martinique and Guadeloupe, while St. Barthélemy and St. Martin are located 130 miles or more north-northwest of Guadeloupe. This small chain plus French Guiana on the South American mainland nearly 1,500 miles to the south-southeast, represents France's remaining heritage in Latin America. Culturally, however, French blood and characteristics may be recognized in other West Indian islands as witnessed by existing names of places and families.

Close relationship of Martinique and Guadeloupe to France goes back to 1635 when the islands came under its control. Sugar was introduced soon after, spelling financial success for two centuries. Slaves, essential to the maintenance of sugar plantations, were brought in from Africa, but the total number never overwhelmed the white population as was the case in French Saint-Domingue (later Haiti). Other factors, too, helped to foster the loyalty of the islands toward the mother country. The colonial policy was never as rough-shod as in some West Indian areas, even though on Guadeloupe the Carib Indians were decimated in the early days of

* The little island of St. Martin, nestled among the northernmost of the Lesser Antilles, belongs half to France and half to the Netherlands, the latter under the name of Sint Maarten.

colonization. Constitutionally, at least, all of the islanders were equal. In addition, they did have representation in French affairs, although by present standards it was not very effective. Finally, the residents took pride in the *haute culture* inherent in the French way of living passed along to them from across the sea.

Before 1946 each of the two islands had a colonial governor who acted on behalf of the Ministry of France Overseas. Martinique and Guadeloupe were colonies in a true sense of the word. But since the constitution of that date both islands have enjoyed the status of overseas departments. Prefects and other officials act through their respective ministries as would be done in any *département* in France, such as Seine-et-Oise or Vaucluse. While local autonomy is assured under this system, it is quite possible that the two West Indian departments have problems quite unlike those of departments close to the Parisian administration. Civil policies for an environment such as Northwest Europe could be somewhat askew from those best suited to tropical islands.

Soft Environment—Harsh Features. Martinique, the size of a typical small midwestern county, has a relief generally more rugged than the Appalachians. Mt. Pelée, in the north, rises to 4,554 feet and has the most formidable volcanic history in the entire West Indian archipelago if not in the Western Hemisphere. In 1902 a single blast of steam from this mountain destroyed the city of St. Pierre, killing 40,000 people and devastating a tenth of the entire island in a few moments. The latest eruption was in 1929.

Guadeloupe, a fourth again as large as Martinique, is actually a double island, the two parts separated by a narrow water passage. The western segment, Basse Terre ("Low Land"), is actually the rugged part of the ensemble, with a peak 4,869 feet high, the highest point in the Lesser Antilles. The eastern segment, Grande Terre ("Large Land"), also belies its meaning, for it is smaller and low-lying, with a maximum elevation of only 450 feet.

By reason of the constantly blowing northeast Trade Winds both islands have modified temperatures with no real extremes but with an abundant rainfall. Located midway along the curve of the Lesser

Antilles, they are menaced by hurricanes, the latest serious one in 1928 destroying plantations and buildings.

As in earlier days sugar dictates the economy of the French islands. Molasses, rum, and alcohol as well as unrefined cane sugar figure prominently as exports extracted from the crop. The rich soil in lowland areas also favors many other tropical crops, of which bananas, coffee, cacao, and pineapple also leave the islands.

The Human Element. Martinique and Guadeloupe each have a population of a little more than a quarter of a million. The resulting densities (on the order of 500 persons per square mile), while not inordinately high, reflect a considerable pressure of population in the arable lowland areas. Cities are not impressively large, though Martinique's capital city, Fort-de-France, has about one-sixth of that island's inhabitants. Basse Terre, the capital of Guadeloupe, located on the west coast, has little more than one-twentieth of the island's total population, but St. Pierre, the leading commercial center, more centrally located, is more than double this size.

The great proportion of the people on both islands are Negroes, or with strong negroid characteristics. Contrary to trends in other parts of the West Indies the population for a time decreased appreciably since 1946. When the islands were drawn into the French Union in that year as departments, many Negroes were free to go —and did go—to France in search of greater opportunities.

As in French areas throughout the world, the culture, including the language, makes a strong imprint upon the local scene. Such traits are readily recognizable in Martinique and Guadeloupe cities, setting them off from other islands in the Lesser Antilles which may otherwise have similar physical characteristics. American tourists always delight at having Fort-de-France or Pointe-à-Pitre on their cruise or flight itinerary in order to drink a "demi" of Beaujolais at their meals and purchase a flagon of Chanel No. 5 as a remembrance.

THE Netherlands Antilles form an integral part of the Kingdom of the Netherlands. Along with Surinam on the South American mainland, they make up one unit of a partnership with the right to manage their own internal affairs.* Nationals living in the Netherlands Antilles have the status of Dutchmen. Great distances from Amsterdam and The Hague along with a total population less than 4 percent (Netherlands Antilles and Surinam combined) as great as the Netherlands proper make the partnership one-sided in some of its aspects. For example, in the Kingdom parliament the Netherlands Antilles, either with Surinam or independently, has less than 10 percent of the total vote. Likewise, the islands depend upon the Dutch navy for defense, contributing a share of the expense. Thus, the autonomy implied in kingdom status, while complete in local affairs, lacks effectiveness in international matters.

Factor of Location. The five and a half islands constituting the Netherlands Antilles cover an area of only 371 square miles, well under one-fourth the size of Long Island. The principal three, Aruba, Bonaire, and Curaçao, popularly known as the ABC islands, lie completely within 70 miles of the Venezuelan coast. Accessibility to the oil-rich Maracaibo region augurs well in light of the huge oil refineries which pour out revenue for the islands.

The remaining islands, St. Eustatius, Saba, and the southern part of St. Martin (*Sint Maarten* in the Dutch language), nestle among the northernmost of the Lesser Antilles 500 miles away. This cleav-

---

* Prior to 1962 the partnership was three-way, with Netherlands Guinea also participating before that political entity passed into Indonesian hands.

age of distance alone poses a complex problem in internal government. Curaçao, largest and most important of the islands, has quite naturally been a leader in administrative affairs. Nearby Aruba, with its own oil refinery—at one time the largest in the world—had sufficient wealth to demand political recognition in its own right. Why then should the southern "levant" islands subsidize the tiny, faraway "windward" islands? This unhappy situation has caused hard feelings on both sides. The best solution to date has been separate local governments for each of the southern islands and a combined one for the northern group.

Resources from Without. In physical resources all of the islands leave much to be desired. Small dimensions plus lack of windward slopes of appreciable extent mean that but little moisture is wrung from the passing Trade Winds. Average rainfall in the Leewards totals no more than 22 inches annually, extremely low for the Caribbean region, and droughts may endure for three months. Little wonder that these islands were not contested in the early colonial grab for plantation sites. Without importing Venezuelan oil to refine, Curaçao and Aruba would be little more than small semi-desert islands; they would stand to be largely bypassed by the stream of Caribbean events as is now true of Bonaire.

Few political entities depend upon a single commodity as completely as do the Netherlands Antilles. The entire agricultural economy is small and desultory, while the only exploited mineral resource consists of phosphate deposits on Curaçao. Petroleum and petroleum products make up 99 percent of the exports and 88 percent of the imports. Since 1920 an economy has evolved, based upon the refining and handling of oil in relatively colossal amounts (36,175,000 metric tons exported in 1961), which places living standards in the Dutch islands among the highest in the entire Caribbean region. But herein also lies a serious danger: political, economic, or even physical change could throw this operation out of balance and diminish the revenue which largely supports the entire economic structure of the Netherlands Antilles. In fact, the government faces several unpleasant realities. Already in evidence, the big oil refineries have "streamlined" their activities, thus requiring less labor. Re-

fineries have been built on Venezuelan soil, and nationalistic tend-
encies plus economic expediency can at any time constrict the flow
of crude oil to Curaçao and Aruba. The unemployment situation
has grown critical. As a result, much emphasis is being given to the
establishment of new industries based on such government-sponsored
advantages as tax concessions as well as the natural advantage of an
excellent site for shipping. The response has been the installation of
chemical plants for the manufacture of commercial fertilizers, a
much-needed commodity in many Caribbean lands and nearby
South America.

The same drive for economic diversity also includes steps toward
developing tourism. Despite a shortage of natural scenery, entice-
ments appear in the form of good beaches, luxury hotels, and convenient travel connections for visitors.

Social Transition.   In a few decades the inhabitants of the Netherlands Antilles have risen from a poverty-ridden society—even by
West Indian standards—to one of relative well being in some ways
approaching sophistication. Before 1924 large numbers of the men
emigrated to find work. Now the industrial complexes for refining
oil on Aruba and Curaçao create a metropolitan air about those
islands, a marked advance from the former simple life dependent
upon the most meager of agricultural pursuits along with some
shipping activities such as bunkering fuel oil and coal. The Dutch
have responded to the newly found prosperity, not only by political
acceptance of their former half-forgotten possession, but in promoting the welfare of the people. For example, much attention is given
to education. The school population exceeds one-fourth of the total
for the islands.

The racial stock of the Netherlands Antilles defies neat character-
ization. Predominately of African origin, it has nevertheless seen
much mixture as peoples from Europe and elsewhere in the Caribbean filtered into the area. On Aruba there remains a rare island of
descendants of the fierce Carib aborigines. More recently, the principal arrivals have been the Dutch and other Westerners as techni-
cians and supervisors for the petroleum refining activities.

Languages spoken in the islands reflect the heterogenous population. Although Dutch is obviously official, English and Spanish are used widely. Local languages, too, have a prominent place among the less literate inhabitants: Papamiento, a dialect composed of both European and African words; and "Creole" English, hard for the average American to recognize. Many people are multilingual.

The rather uncertain economic future of the Netherlands Antilles places the population in an unenviable position of having to face retrogression in living standards. If the oil stops flowing, the natural resources of the area itself cannot possibly support the inhabitants in the manner to which they have become accustomed.

15 *Outlying Areas of the United States*

Puerto Rico acquired commonwealth status in 1952, aptly termed in Spanish as *Estado Libre Associado* (Free Associated State). The island maintains a voluntary association with the United States and at the same time rules itself with an autonomous form of representative government. There is a minority faction in Puerto Rico which clamors for complete independence and another advocating statehood after the example of Alaska and Hawaii. But the great majority of the people prefer the status they hold and so express themselves by staunchly supporting Governor Muñoz Marin and the Popular Democratic party which brought the present situation about.

Before the day of the Commonwealth all was not so well. A long, hard fight was waged by spirited Puerto Ricans for the recognition they desired for their island. In turn, the United States government, even with the best of intentions toward their possession, paced political development very slowly. Ill-advised controls, the power of commercial interests, and the appointment of governors unsympathetic to Puerto Rican aspirations all were blocks in the path of progress. The depression in the 1930's, bad in the United States, posed even greater economic strains on the insular colony. In the long run, however, the depression undoubtedly gave incentive to resolve the grave problems at the root of an impractical political economy. In its wake came World War II and attendant economic stimulation which stimulated employment by activating construction. Ultimately the great source of strength for a rejuvenated

Puerto Rico came with "Operation Bootstrap," in which the United States and her dependency alike worked toward a full-scale accord on the political, economic, and social fronts.

Insular Compactness. Puerto Rico possesses less than one-third the area of Maryland, considered to be one of our smaller states. Yet on its 3,421 square miles the island offers a dynamic physical environment of great diversity. Rectangular in shape, it measures about 100 miles east and west and 36 miles north and south. Extending lengthwise through the island, a small cordillera-like backbone rises to altitudes comparable to the Blue Ridge Mountains of Virginia. To both the north and south a hilly belt parallels the higher land. Finally, rimming the island, a coastal lowland belt occupies slightly over one-fourth of the total area and gives Puerto Ricans their most fertile agricultural area.

Although the climate is basically tropical, the thermometer has recorded differences through an absolute range of 64 Fahrenheit degrees, from 39° in the mountainous interior to 103° on the coastal plain. Rainfall statistics reveal much greater annual extremes, from 188 inches on a northern windward slope to less than 30 inches on the south coast in the lee of the mountains. Because of such physical variations the Puerto Rican landscape ranges from tropical rain-forest to dry lowland incapable of supporting profitable crops without irrigation.

In material natural resources Puerto Ricans count the approximately one-fourth of their land that is highly productive agriculturally and a climate extremely favorable to vegetative growth. Beyond this ultrashort list, however, the resource inventory becomes a meager one. Mineral deposits, even though present in variety, generally do not warrant commercial exploitation. Especially unfortunate is the absence of mineral fuels. Only such common items as sand, gravel, clay, and building stone are to be found in adequate supply.

The ample rainfall does permit development of hydroelectric energy, but full potential has now been realized, leaving no opportunity for future expansion. Forests have largely been cleared to make way for the ~~plow.~~ More optimistic, estimates for a fishing

plough

industry in Puerto Rican waters give hope for providing more sea-food for local demand and for export.

The three small islands of Vieques, Mona, and Culebra, known collectively as "outlying Puerto Rico," extend the Commonwealth's territory east and west another 50 miles. Difficult of access and lack-ing a physical resource base of any significant potential, these bits of land (totaling 80 square miles) have long been in the backwater of economic development. Recently, however, an offshore location in a tropical environment has attracted two activities to Vieques: underwater defense training, and skin diving as a sport.

An Animated Population. The 1960 census showed 2,353,297 people to be living in Puerto Rico, nearly two and a half times the number in 1899 when the island became a U.S. dependency. More people live in Puerto Rico than in Oklahoma, a state with 20 times as much space. In fact, the Commonwealth's population density of 687 persons per square mile is comparable to that of industrial sectors in New England and the Middle Atlantic states. One scholar computed that if conterminous United States were as densely popu-lated as Puerto Rico the number of inhabitants would exceed one-half the present world's total population. Nothing better to do I suppose

High population density exerts a pressure upon Puerto Rico's land, especially since the economy depends primarily upon agricul-tural production. Approximately 1,850 persons must rely upon each square mile of arable land, or nearly three to each acre. In the United States, excluding Alaska, this ratio is reversed—more than three acres of arable land for each person.

Crowding over the Puerto Rican landscape is evident to anyone who has ever driven past the countless small farm homes scattered wherever there may be a bit of land to cultivate. One wonders why there is no terracing in a country where nearly three fourths of the land is classified as highlands or rolling hills, as is so common in many other crowded areas in the world. Dr. Rafael Pico,* leading

---

* Dr. Rafael Pico has been a principal participant in a major land use survey in Puerto Rico and has written extensively on this and other subjects relative to the geography of the island. At present he is president of the Government Development Bank for Puerto Rico.

Puerto Rican geographer, was asked just this question. His answer, paraphrased, was:

> To justify terracing labor must be extremely inexpensive, as under relatively primitive conditions; and there must be a long tradition of a heavy population to condition people to the backbreaking toil of establishing and maintaining terraced agriculture. Puerto Rico does not qualify in either instance. Also there is and always has been good level land available for intensive cultivation.

Percent by percent the relation of urban to rural population increases. In 1960 dwellers in cities of 2,500 or more inhabitants exceeded 44 percent, comparable to the situation in the states of Arkansas, Kentucky, and South Carolina. As might be expected, San Juan and Ponce, the two leading cities, show substantial growth, the former now a metropolitan area in the true American sense, exceeding 600,000 in population.

For nearly half a century migration to the United States has been a means of alleviating population pressure in Puerto Rico. A slow trickle at first, the outward flow increased to tens of thousands by the late 1940's. After a record exodus of 75,000 in 1953 the emigration movement tapered off. In addition, large numbers of Puerto Ricans began to return to their native island until now the movement into and out of the island more or less balances. Presently, with three-quarters of a million Puerto Ricans in New York City, plus large groups in other major eastern cities, there is a lively traffic back and forth between the Continent and the Commonwealth. Twenty scheduled commercial airline flights daily in each direction amount to miniature migrations in themselves. Many of the flights are "air buses" or "thrift expresses" with special low fares which stimulate this type of travel. Greater economic opportunities at home in recent years have in part at least accounted for this rather strange two-way traffic. It is assuredly novel to find young Puerto Ricans in small cities who know the labyrinth of New York's subways better than they do the contours of the mountains surrounding their native home.

Continental-Insular Partnership. Despite a modest resource base and in the face of a rapidly expanding population a partnership between Puerto Rico and the United States has paid high dividends. Instead of a miserable, overcrowded island full of poverty-stricken peasants—which it could be—Puerto Rico now has a place in the sun.

The partnership works in both directions. Association with the United States means much to the Puerto Ricans. Of paramount significance, they have the advantage of a colossal market relatively close at hand. They can draw upon technical skills to any degree. The mainland is likewise a source of capital for investment in island industries. In short, Puerto Ricans make the most of the political affiliation by aligning their economy with the American system.

In turn, the United States can point with pride to this outlying area where democracy thrives. As a showplace it serves as an example to the world, especially poignant in light of its location in the Caribbean—an area not replete with success stories of economic and political stability. Less abstract benefits also derive from the close alignment, amounting to a source of products from an exotic environment and opportunities for investment with minimum risk over an expanded area.

Without trade restrictions some 90 percent of the Commonwealth's exports and imports are with the United States. Many problems remain to be worked out, but they seem to daunt neither continent nor Puerto Rico.

Balanced Economy. Before 1940 the economic welfare of Puerto Rico depended primarily upon the success of marketing agricultural crops, particularly sugar. The shortcomings in Cuba's one-crop system were found here, though on a lesser scale. Reforms in the system of land tenure, activated by the Popular Democratic Party, began a sequence of improvements in the island's agricultural pattern. Later a thorough rural land classification program further stimulated the improvement of agriculture, eventually eradicating the gloom of destitution which had long been hanging over the Puerto Rican landscape. The typical farmer, either landowner or tenant, is no longer subjugated to the interests of large landowners. With confidence he grows sugar cane, coffee, tobacco, and fruit crops, all of which figure prominently in the Commonwealth's commercial production. Further, he enjoys such advantages as sharing in the profits of his labor and raising food crops for his family's use.

Agriculture alone could not bring prosperity to Puerto Rico. Much attention was focused upon the development of industries in order to build a balanced economy. The processing and manufacturing of agricultural products were obviously one phase of the program, but plans also called for many types of plants. In all instances Puerto Ricans utilized the advantages they did possess to produce commodities which would gain favor in an export market or which would yield items more cheaply than to import them. For example, many textile establishments employ Puerto Ricans for their handiwork, materials being sent to the island expressly for this skill and later exported as finished goods. As a result of the determined drive toward industrialism, hundreds of factories, some of them branches of American manufacturing concerns, are scattered over the island. Many have been located in the smaller cities in order to tap a new labor supply. Employment in them goes a long way toward taking up the slack of surplus labor common in an agricultural economy.

Puerto Rico's industrial growth carries with it many advantages other than the factories themselves. To mention a few, hydroelectric plants were constructed to run the plants and to provide household current; service functions were needed for the thousands of new employees; and low-cost housing developments were required in industrial districts.

The Modern Look. Enlightened leadership and hard work have given Puerto Rico a "new look." It is readily apparent to all who visit the island and see the enthusiastic attitude of the people. It can also be measured objectively by observing the mounting per capita income, increasing production statistics, an impressively low death rate, and other figures denoting advance. Bulldozers effectively write off shanty towns as new modern-looking living quarters rise.

An excellent highway net covers the island, no point really suffers from isolation. Supermarkets, smart shops, and other symbols of the new American cityscape have now taken root in Puerto Rico.

VIRGIN ISLANDS OF THE UNITED STATES

From the eastern coast of Puerto Rico on a clear day one may see the outline of St. Thomas in the Virgin Islands, only 40 miles away. Paradoxically, the Virgin Island group (including the British Virgin Islands) forms the westernmost part of the Lesser Antilles but structurally belongs to the Greater Antilles. This position implies that the islands constitute an insular junction, and it is in this role that St. Thomas was an important coaling station during the days of steamships.

Strategic location again shows up in the history of the Virgin Island group. In 1917 the United States, after half a century of negotiations, purchased the islands from Denmark for $25 million —at $259 per acre certainly no bargain from the standpoint of land surface alone.

Before World War II, Virgin Islanders depended largely upon marginal agriculture for their livelihood. Rough St. Thomas, relatively level but rain-poor St. Croix, and tiny St. John together made up the three units of what some called America's Caribbean "poorhouse." But the pleasant climate has recently won out in attracting a bumper crop of tourists to the islands. Eighteen plane loads of eager Americans pour into St. Thomas from San Juan each day, anxious to buy duty-free merchandise, some staying overnight at the luxury hotels.

16 *Politico-Socio-Economic Dilemma*

STRENGTHS and weaknesses within the West Indian area reflect in kind upon the United States and its status as world community. Close proximity makes political and economic situations in the Caribbean of direct concern to American interests. Social conditions here will always serve as a barometer and may act as a catalyst to the area's progress or retrogression. Thus, the United States looks to and deals with the people of the various islands and entities as a means of advancing regional stability.

The strategic aspects of national defense in the United States hinge in part upon political machinations taking place in what long has been a Latin American proving ground. Economic well-being in the same area, while not vital to the tissue of American commerce, does insure a much-needed viability for hemispheric solidarity. At the very least, the area at our southeastern doorstep must receive highest priority in attention given to international matters and in any attempts made to understand areas beyond our own borders. Intelligent action necessarily must follow intelligent evaluation, whether by government or private citizens.

In the face of a population explosion and often under political pressures which defy cold economic logic, how can the West Indian islanders demand the best possible government for themselves? What can they do to upgrade their living standards? Or in any event how can they preserve a feeling of hope and assurance of better things to come within their social environment? Without economic viability social issues become clouded and political stabil-

ity tends to disintegrate. Acute problems become national crises
which directly encompass the United States and European as well
as Caribbean governments. How they are handled determines to
a large extent how the islands fare. Puerto Rico by a vigorous, constructive program has been able to build confidence in itself and
attain sharp material successes; Cuba by keying economic measures
to a political system with heedless abandon of geography has recently taken up rationing. Jamaica and Trinidad and Tobago op-
timistically gird for the future under the aegis of the Commonwealth; Haiti must cope with ever greater problems under the
strain of a highly personalized regime which has declared its inten-
tion to perpetuate itself indefinitely.

An indication of the economic status of the various islands may
be read into the per capita incomes.* All are extremely low in comparison with that of the United States and considerably less than
those of the countries of Western Europe. Within the archipelago
the variance is likewise great, the highest being approximately eight
times that of the lowest. Puerto Rico and Trinidad and Tobago
would appear to have the top living standards of the area, with per
capita incomes of about $700 and $500 respectively. At the bottom
of the heap, Haiti's inhabitants each earn on the average only $85
per annum. Immediately prior to the revolution Cuba's per capita
income stood at $340.

In analyzing the ills of West Indian economy the adverse factors
which come to the fore tend to be so constant from island to island
that they sound almost like clichés. Without exhausting the list,
four of these relentless handicaps suffice to illustrate the challenges
facing West Indian leadership:

(1) Population pressures crowd, if they do not outdistance, material economic gain;

(2) Commodity prices on the world market, upon which island
economies must depend, fluctuate much like a wheel of chance;

* Per capita income figures for comparative purposes are necessarily estimates because of the irregularity of the statistics in methods of computation
and in time.

(3) Political instability, underlain with dissenting internal factions, often paces economic chaos; and

(4) Unfortunately for the West Indies, the world continues to become a more expensive place in which to live, a trend of particular concern in less developed areas which in their feeble way must try to compete with countries more advanced technically. For example, sugar production in Barbados has increased ten-fold in the last century and a quarter, and at the same time the quality has improved. Sugar comprises 80 percent of the island's exports. Yet despite the fact that during the same period the population has little more than doubled the economy continues to be depressed.

No ready answer is at hand with which to resolve these perplexing problems. Rather, a wide range of measures has been adopted —not always systematically—to alleviate the economic ills. Social improvement, being less readily identifiable, lags, while political evils may be so deeply ingrained that they are self-perpetuating. Nevertheless, one can tick off items in the inventory of steps taken to give the West Indian islands their rightful place in a competitive world:

(1) Promotion and programming of industrialization by tax holidays and other devices; little-developed industries, as pastoral, forestry, and fishing, may also be encouraged;

(2) Stimulation of tourism;

(3) Capitalization of specialized production, including improvement of the quality of commodities to be exported;

(4) Diversification of production insofar as feasible to lessen dependence on imports;

(5) Encouragement of commercial alliances to facilitate favorable trade relations;

(6) Increasing use of birth control methods; and

(7) Acceptance or encouragement of regulated migration to relieve unemployment.

Not one or two, but all remedial actions possible are required to combat problems and improve standards in the West Indian scene. To stimulate progress the areas of associated sovereignty including dependencies have cooperation and sponsorship from the metropole. All islands are recipients, either actual or potential, of economic assistance stemming from the United States and Europe. Finally, the Alliance for Progress program encompasses the Dominican Republic and Haiti as signatories of the Punta Del Este Charter. Any success enjoyed by this broad venture "to bring a better life to all the peoples of the Americas" must necessarily create an improved economic climate for the entire Caribbean realm.

Appendix

TABLE 1

Population Growth of the West Indies

ISLAND OR POLITICAL ENTITY	POPULATION in thousands			Average Annual % of Increase 1953-59 [2]
	1960	1940	1920 [1]	
INDEPENDENT STATES				
Cuba	6,797	4,566	3,945 [3]	2.1
Dominican Republic	2,994	1,674	879	3.5
Haiti	3,505	2,751	2,124	1.2
Jamaica	1,607	1,212	855	1.8 [4]
Trinidad and Tobago	832	476	389	3.0 [4]
BRITISH ISLANDS				
Antigua	61	34	30	1.9 [5]
Bahamas	105	70	61 [6]	9.6 [4]
Barbados	232	179	155 [7]	1.3
Cayman Islands	8	7	5 [7]	0.8 [5]
Dominica	60	52	41	1.6 [5]
Grenada	89	76	66 [7]	1.5 [5]
Montserrat	12	15	12	—1.2 [5]
St. Kitts Nevis and Anguilla	57	43	38 [7]	1.5 [5]
St. Lucia	86	70	52 [7]	1.5 [5]
St. Vincent	80	61	44	1.9 [5]
Turks and Caicos	6	6	6 [7]	—0.4 [5]
Virgin Islands, British	7	7	5	0.9
FRENCH ISLANDS				
Guadeloupe	270	190 [8]	—	2.8
Martinique	277	209 [8]	244 [7]	2.5
DUTCH ISLANDS				
Netherlands Antilles	190	107	55	1.5

131

U.S. AREAS

Puerto Rico	2,358	1,880	1,312	1.0
Virgin Islands, United States	32	25	22 [6]	—

TOTAL POPULATION 19,665

[1] U.N. Statistical Papers, Series A, Vol. XIII, No. 4, *Population and Vital Statistics Report,* 1961.

[2] 1953-59 data from *U.N. Demographic Yearbook,* 1960; 1953-57 data from *Statistical Abstract of Latin America,* 1960, Center of Latin American Studies, U.C.L.A., 1960; 1946-60 data from Table I, *The West Indian Federation,* D. Lowenthal, editor, American Geographical Society, 1961.

[3] 1931.

[4] 1953-57.

[5] 1946-60.

[6] 1930.

[7] 1921.

[8] 1946.

TABLE 2

Area and Population by Sovereignty in the West Indies

Sovereign Unit	Area (Sq. Mi.)	Population (See Note)	Date
Cuba	44,218	7,203,000	7/63
Dominican Republic	18,704	3,334,000	7/63
Haiti	10,714	4,448,000	6/63
Jamaica	4,411	1,684,000	6/63
Trinidad and Tobago	1,980	880,000	6/62
British West Indies	6,108	828,000	12/62
French West Indies	1,118	586,000	7/62
Netherlands Antilles	371	200,000	1/63
Outlying Areas of U.S.	3,576	2,580,000	10/63
Total	91,200	21,743,000	

NOTE: Population figures are based upon the official U.N. estimates as of the dates in the last column, with the following exceptions: Antigua, Cayman Islands, St. Vincent, Trinidad and Tobago, British Virgin Islands, and Virgin Islands of the United States, 7/62; St. Lucia, 6/62.

TABLE 3

Identification of Sovereign Units in the West Indies

CUBA

Includes Isle of Pines (1,181 sq. mi.) and some 1,600 offshore islands

DOMINICAN REPUBLIC

Includes Saona, Beata, and several other small offshore islands

HAITI

Includes several offshore islands of which the largest are Gonave (254 sq. mi.), Tortue (70 sq. mi.), and Vache (20 sq. mi.)

JAMAICA

No offshore islands of importance; Turks and Caicos and Cayman Islands no longer attached to Jamaica as dependencies

TRINIDAD AND TOBAGO

Made up of Trinidad (1,864 sq. mi.) and Tobago (116 sq. mi.)

BRITISH WEST INDIES

Made up of 12 colonies as follows:

1. *Antigua* (171 sq. mi.)
   Consists of three islands: Antigua (108 sq. mi.), Barbuda (62 sq. mi.), and Redonda (1 sq. mi.)
2. *Bahamas* (4,404 sq. mi.)
   Group of some 700 islands and cays of which 20 are inhabited. Most important are: Acklins Is. (120 sq. mi.), Andros (1,600 sq. mi.), Crooked Is. (76 sq. mi.), Eleuthera (164 sq. mi.), Exuma (100 sq. mi.), Grand Bahama (430 sq. mi.), Great and Little Inagua (560 sq. mi.), Great and Small Abaco (776 sq. mi.), Long Is. (130 sq. mi.), Mayaguana (96 sq. mi.), New Providence (58 sq. mi.), San Salvador, or Watlings (60 sq. mi.)
3. *Barbados* (166 sq. mi.) No dependencies
4. *Cayman Islands* (93 sq. mi.)
   Consists of three islands: Grand Cayman (71 sq. mi.), Little Cayman (9 sq. mi.) and Cayman Brac (13 sq. mi.)
5. *Dominica* (305 sq. mi.) No dependencies
6. *Grenada* (133 sq. mi.)
   Consists of the island of Grenada (120 sq. mi.) and the southern Grenadines, including Carriacou (13 sq. mi.), Frigate, Petit Martinique, Petit St. Vincent, and Ronde
7. *Montserrat* (32 sq. mi.) No dependencies
8. *St. Kitts Nevis and Anguilla* (155 sq. mi.)
   Consists of three main islands and one dependency: St. Kitts, or St. Christopher (68 sq. mi.), Nevis (50 sq. mi.), Anguilla (35 sq. mi.), and Sombrero (2 sq. mi.)

9. *St. Lucia* (238 sq. mi.) No dependencies
10. *St. Vincent* (150 sq. mi.)
   Consists of the island of St. Vincent (133 sq. mi.) and the northern Grenadines, including Baliceaux, Battowia, Bequia (7 sq. mi.), Canouan, Mayreau, Mustique, Petit Mustique, Quatre, Savau, Tobago Cays, and Union
11. *Turks and Caicos* (202 sq. mi.)
   Consists of two groups: Turks include Grand Turk (9 sq. mi.), Salt Cay and Ambergris Cay; Caicos include North Caicos (54 sq. mi.), East Caicos, Middle, or Grand, Caicos (73 sq. mi.), South Caicos (9 sq. mi.), West Caicos (10 sq. mi.), and Blue Hills, or Providenciales (42 sq. mi.)
12. *Virgin Islands* (59 sq. mi.)
   Includes Anegada (13 sq. mi.), Jost Van Dyke, Peter, Tortola (21 sq. mi.), Virgin Gorda, and a number of secondary islands

FRENCH WEST INDIES

   Made up of two French departments as follows:
1. *Guadeloupe* (687 sq. mi.)
   Consists of the island of Guadeloupe (583 sq. mi.) and several dependencies: Marie Galante (58 sq. mi.), La Désirade (10 sq. mi.), Les Saintes (6 sq. mi.), Petit Terre (1 sq. mi.), St. Barthélemy (10 sq. mi.), and part of St. Martin (20 sq. mi.)
2. *Martinique* (431 sq. mi.) No dependencies

NETHERLANDS ANTILLES

   Made up of five islands and part of a sixth: Aruba (68 sq. mi.), Bonaire (98 sq. mi.), Curaçao (174 sq. mi.), Saba (5 sq. mi.), St. Eustatius (7 sq. mi.), and part of St. Martin (13 sq. mi.)

OUTLYING AREAS OF THE UNITED STATES

   Made up of the Commonwealth of Puerto Rico, the Virgin Islands, and several possessions:
1. *Puerto Rico* (3,435 sq. mi.)
   Offshore islands include Vieques (51 sq. mi.), Mono (19 sq. mi.), Culebra (11 sq. mi.), and Desecheo
2. *Virgin Islands* (133 sq. mi.)
   Consists of three main islands: St. Croix (82 sq. mi.), St. John (19 sq. mi.), and St. Thomas (27 sq. mi.)
3. *Other Outlying Areas*
   Consist of Corn Islands (4 sq. mi.), Navassa (2 sq. mi.), Swan Islands (1 sq. mi.), and Quita Sueno, Roncador, and Serraña Banks

Bibliography

Books:

Canet, Gerardo, *Atlas de Cuba,* Harvard University Press, Cambridge, 1949.

Hanson, Earl Parker, *Puerto Rico: Ally for Progress,* A Searchlight Original, Van Nostrand, Princeton, 1962.

Lowenthal, David, editor, *The West Indies Federation,* American Geographical Society, New York, 1961.

Picó, Rafael, *Puerto Rico: Planificación y Acción,* Banco Gubernamental de Fomento Para Puerto Rico, San Juan, 1962.

Starkey, Otis P., *The Economic Geography of Barbados,* Columbia University Press, New York, 1939.

Willey, Gordon Randolph, *Middle American Anthropology,* Pan American Union, Washington, 1958.

Miscellaneous Publications:

Agency for International Development, Washington, D.C.: Statistics and Reports on West Indian areas.

American Geographical Society, New York, "Focus": Issues on various West Indian countries.

Institute of Caribbean Studies, University of Puerto Rico, Rio Piedras: "Caribbean Studies," published since 1961.

Office of Naval Research, Washington, D.C.: Reports based on field work on various areas in the British West Indies and Trinidad.

Pan American Union, Washington, D.C.: Series of pamphlets on Cuba, Dominican Republic, and Haiti.

Service de Presse et d'Information, Ambassade de France, New York: Material on Guadeloupe and Martinique.

Special Operations Research Office, American University, Washington, D.C.: "Special Warfare Area Handbook for Cuba," 1961.

——— "Case Studies in Insurgency and Revolutionary Warfare," 1963.

Index of Places